Praying
for **Freckles**

Praying
for **Freckles**
Growing Up Maronite in Pittsburgh's Hill District

by Gene Kail
Foreword by Samuel Hazo

Lambing Press
Pittsburgh

For Aunt Martha

*who stayed the longest and
put up with the most*

Table of Contents

Foreword

By Samuel Hazo

G ene Kail approaches the creation of this historical and social narrative both professionally and personally. His focus is on an area in Pittsburgh, known as "the Hill" or "the Hill District," that was immediately adjacent to Downtown Pittsburgh and was populated by people of twenty-five different ethnicities. (It was featured years later in the hit TV program "Hill Street Blues.")

He describes individuals (his parents and family especially, as well as their contemporaries) not only for their place in the history of the Hill, but personally for the invaluable contributions they made to his life and the lives of his contemporaries.

He knew and knows his subjects, describes them in context, and lets them come to life and speak for themselves, often in broken English. And he never loses his sense of humor, which is of tremendous value in this kind of historical narrative. It's more than humdrum sociology.

In this context I find resonances with aspects of my own family's history. My grandfather John Abdou emigrated from Saida to Pittsburgh in the early years of the twentieth century. Before the first decade ended, he had brought his wife, his son and daughter, two brothers, his sister and his mother to his then home on the Hill.

Because my mother and my aunt had contracted a form of conjunctivitis on Ellis Island, there was talk of returning them to Lebanon. Knowing that this was impossible, since there was no longer a family there to return to, my grandfather wrote a letter to then President Theodore Roosevelt on their behalf. It must have been quite a persuasive letter because Roosevelt then ordered the immediate release of these two young girls to my grandfather, who then brought them to Pittsburgh. My mother, Lottie Abdou, excelled at Epiphany School to such a degree that the priest in charge (Father Lawrence O'Connell) involved her in teaching other immigrant children the American language. Later, along with my grandfather's sister, Katherine Abdou, she became a nurse and became fluent in English, Arabic, and Greek.

After marrying my father, she often accompanied herself on the lute and sang at family and public gatherings to such acclaim that the prime pianist with the New York Philharmonic invited her to New York to record her songs. When she died, my brother and I were still under six years of age. Because my father made his living by traveling, my Aunt Katherine in effect raised us, personifying the kind of courage and self-sacrifice that only her genuine love for my mother can explain. She never looked for applause or praise for doing so. It was simply the way that life's reversals should be faced, and she did what she did lovingly and heroically.

Mr. Kail's reference to the importance of Maronite Catholicism to these new Americans and their children parallels the devotion of numerous other immigrants to their respective rites and reveals the invaluable importance that such devotion had for them. There were times in the lives of all of them when their religious beliefs were all they had.

Black families had lived on the Hill from the time of the Emancipation, creating a formidable legacy in music and other arts, and they were followed at the turn of the century by newcomers from Italy and Syria (particularly that part of Syria that became Lebanon in the mid-1940's), as well as a number of Jewish families. This population intermingled, but each segment clung to its old-country or ethnic traditions for as long as possible. It was a living, viable neighborhood.

The Hill District so described lasted until the late-1950s when commercial and civic interests, under the mandate of eminent domain and urban renewal, eliminated it block by block, family by family.

It should be noted that the immigrant complexion of the Hill constituted a distinct change from Pittsburgh's nineteenth-century character. Welsh, Scotch-Irish, and German immigrants dominated and directed civic life in the wake of the Industrial Revolution. Newcomers from Eastern Europe followed and actually became the laborers who worked in the steel mills. After the turn of the century the incoming Italian (mostly from Calabria) and Syrian (later called "Lebanese") immigrants came to escape from poverty or, in the case of the Levantines, the Ottomans.

The Italians were craftsmen of various skills — landscapers, and construction workers (the beautiful stone homes in Mt. Lebanon — which coincidentally was named after Lebanon by a Protestant clergyman who had ministered there — were made from stone cut and honed predominantly by Italian stonecutters and masons). One surviving shoemaker told me recently that at one time there were two hundred shoemakers, mostly from Italy, in Pittsburgh, but that they had dwindled to fewer than twenty. The Levantines became small-shop owners, businessmen, restaurateurs, peddlers, or employees in various branches of local government.

It is a cliché to say that the United States is a nation of immigrants, but it should be said, regardless, to underscore the importance of immigration in the ongoing history of the country. Each immigrant group retained and retains its own characteristics, but as Americans they transform or discard what they no longer see as relevant to their lives. This is inevitable. There is a generational change when an immigrant living in America becomes spiritually an American whose forbears were immigrants. As one who lived and lives this legacy, Gene Kail writes of it with humor, understanding, insight, respect and love.

Introduction

Every family has family stories. Not every family has someone to tell them. Which is just as well. If everyone was off writing family stories, who would remain to read mine?

Actually, many families have a person in whom the family history resides; but, as long as it remains oral rather than cast in some more permanent form, it remains ephemeral and in danger of disappearing.

The stories in this book are not just my stories. They are my family's stories. They do not exist without the family. Therefore, in some ways, I am merely borrowing them. In all honesty, they probably tell the basic story of a lot of families — from immigration to assimilation — especially where I grew up. They have been told, adapted and amended, burnished and shared over many years, so they're ready for prime time.

Since the book is about family, and I want to keep mine, it says little about the dark moments that permeate the history of any family. Rather, I wanted to celebrate the moments that, for me, defined the real nature of "family values." On the other hand, there are bound to be people who become upset after reading parts of this book. It might be someone I included or didn't; something I said, or didn't; something I remembered, or didn't. For anyone who gets upset at what I say in the book, I can only say, with all sincerity, "Get over it!"

You might consider it presumptuous of me to assume there is an audience for my family stories. My family has always fascinated my friends, and the friends of all of my siblings. While admittedly anecdotal in nature, this market research is good enough for me. Besides, my family reproduces like rabbits. If only some of each of the current several generations buys/downloads/pirates a copy of the book, it will be a runaway bestseller.

One of the primary reasons I have undertaken this project is to answer questions about the family for myself and subsequent generations. A family needs a context, a history; it needs to be connected at both ends. Otherwise, you are quite literally "disconnected," each generation beginning again, having to create ever again family values and traditions.

Finally, there is the issue of truth. In our family, truth is sometimes a subject for negotiation. Are these family stories true? Who knows?

They should be.

For these stories, and for so many other things, I thank my family.

Gene Kail
October, 2015

Grade school photo --
shows early promise

Chapter One

Basic Principles

Why am I writing my family stories? There are a lot of reasons. For example, the other day, one of my sibling's grandchildren called me Uncle Bob. Since I am Uncle Gene, I decided that my nieces and nephews, and grandnieces and grandnephews, needed to get in touch with their roots. So I had to plant some, quickly.

This chapter merely provides some notes that might be helpful in understanding my family, an advantage I've had to forgo. I didn't have a primer.

The families of both my mother and father emigrated from Lebanon in the late 1800s. My father's family settled in Pittsburgh. By the time I came along, his immediate family consisted of his father (Rashid or Richard), his Aunt Salima and her third husband Tom, his uncle Habib, his brother Joe, and his two sisters, Philomena and Genevieve (also an indeterminate bunch of cousins). His mother had lost several children in the flu epidemics of the early twentieth century, and had died very young in 1936.

My mother's family eventually settled in Cincinnati, and then Dayton, Ohio. By the time I knew them, they consisted of her grandmother, father and mother (Joseph and Bitrosea), her Aunt Irene, and four siblings, Dorothy, Albert, Elias (David), and Martha, as well as a few uncles, aunts and cousins.

To understand my family, you need to realize that my father and his brother married two sisters (not their own, of course), and they all lived in the same house. Among them, they had ten children — in order: Dick, Bob, Gene, Mike, Mariann, Fran, Judy, Rosanne, Theresa and Patty — raised, for the most part, as brothers and sisters, sharing bed, bath, and discipline. We often use the terms "brother," "sister," and "cousin" interchangeably, and we coined the term "sister/ cousin" for situations that demanded greater accuracy.

Thus, although Franny is actually my double first cousin, I often refer to her as my sister, and treat her as such. And while her children are actually my first cousins once removed; and her grandchildren are actually my first cousins twice removed; they all call me Uncle Gene (except for one, who calls me Uncle Bob). Got that straight?

My paternal grandfather Rashid and my unmarried Aunt Philomena also lived with us, along with several friends who often split time between the "boys' bedroom" and their own homes.

Let me illustrate this graphically:

Parent – Parent – Parent – Parent
Kid
Kid
Kid
Kid
Kid
Kid
Kid
Kid
Kid
Kid
Aunt
Grandfather
Friends

I am not exaggerating when I say that someone was always staying over. And, since I had the double bed, I often woke to find a new friend. At one point, my brother Dick's friend Rinky, having run away from home, stayed at our house for several days, sleeping in the boys' room and showing up for meals. (But then, Rinky always showed up for meals.) It wasn't until his mother called to find out if anyone had seen him that he was discovered and sent home.

There are some further insights that are important in understanding my family. Among the parents, there was a rudimentary division of labor. Aunt Martha pretty much ran the household, while my mother (Helen, day shift) and father (Dave, night shift) worked at the family tavern. My Uncle Joe was employed in several capacities:

as a chemist at U.S. Steel, as an insurance salesman, in technical sales, and so on. Interestingly, my dad and Uncle Joe did most of the shopping, and they loved doing it.

We originally lived in Pittsburgh's Hill District, a vibrant community of Lebanese, Italian, Jewish and African-American strains, a mixed neighborhood that worked. I don't mean to imply that racial or ethnic issues were never a problem; but, for the most part, it worked. When they tore down the Hill to redevelop it in the middle fifties, we moved east to what was actually the Soho district but was usually considered part of Oakland.

We are somewhat unique in that all ten of the siblings are still in touch and see each other often. There are tensions and disagreements, but we tend to resolve them, live with them, or ignore them. Many of us, along with children and grandchildren, still meet weekly for Sunday brunch at the family house, held together by my Aunt Martha, who, at the time of this writing, is 93 and still a devil.

As a family, one of the values we prize most highly is hospitality. My father loved to see people eating his food at his table, and all of us love to entertain. Ours was the house where everyone hung out. We made no special fuss about it; you ate what we ate. Our social activities, even with company present, were simple, consisting primarily of card games, quiz games, and conversation.

Since my mother and her sister came from Ohio, there was some local disgruntlement when two of its most eligible bachelors turned their backs on the Pittsburgh community and married into the Dayton community. That "community" was primarily the Maronite Catholic community, in which my Grandfather Rashid was one of the local "patriarchs."

And one final insight that permeates this book, without an understanding of which you might miss much of the point: *Maronites are Catholic. If this seems obvious to you, well, good. It's not obvious to everyone.*

I once dated a brilliant Irish lawyer from a major law firm, who represented several important Catholic clients. She had graduated near the top of her class from Notre Dame Law School. You don't get much more Catholic than that. She tried to be kind, but couldn't mask her doubts about my religious status. It wasn't until I showed her the texts of the new Code of Canon Law for the Eastern Churches that she began to believe.

To this day, I'm not sure she ever fully accepted it.

While I was at Central Catholic High School, the question often arose, especially from the Business Office "Downtown," as it tried to establish tuition policies, whether or not we Maronites should pay "non-Catholic" tuition. Both then and now, I found it difficult to understand this ignorance on the part of otherwise intelligent people, but let me make it clear.

Maronites don't have to grow beards or look fierce; we can eat anything you do; we don't practice arcane rituals to place a curse on our enemies, and we don't do strange things to small animals in the dark. We have no relationship to the Mennonites, the Moravians, or the Masons. We are not "one of the Orthodox churches." So let's get one thing straight from the start.

We, too, are Catholics.

I think that's enough to get you started.

(Well, maybe a *few* arcane rituals.)

Friends over for my birthday party

Chapter Two

Of Roots and Such

Who We Are

My paternal grandfather and my maternal grandmother both told the same story about the origins of the family in Lebanon. Where they got it, I'll never know, since none of their siblings, and only one of their children, ever told the same tale. It seemed to be their exclusive birthright.

It went something like this. My paternal family, upon emigrating from Lebanon, had taken the name "Kail," which seemed to be a bastardization of an Arabic name about eleven inches long. My maternal family took the "house" name as a patronymic. (The "house" to which you belonged, we were told, was very important in Lebanese culture.)

We came from the House of Zennie. It lacked the grandeur of the "House of Hapsburg" or "Windsor," but it was good enough for us. The fact that some of my cousins spelled it "Zenni," "Zeni," or even "Zahennie," simply enriched the brand.

Grampa Rashid maintained that the family originated from a French knight during the Crusades. Grandma Bitrosea told a similar story, as did Uncle Al. The "Knight" was one of Richard's officers, and, after being wounded in battle, was taken in by the village headman, fell in love with the daughter of the house, and stayed to marry her and settle in the village.

To my mind, the tale thus far raised many more questions than it answered. For example, why wasn't the house traced through the maternal line? What was her "house" name? Was he a second or third son, since he seemed to be willing to "leave it all behind"? Was this a great romance, or did he "have to" marry her? And so on. You can see why few answers were forthcoming.

Of course, when my grandfather would tell the story, we

grandchildren, lacking any human sensitivity or sense of history, or even common decency, would tease that the "knight" was probably a French buck private during World War I. Our grandfather would then utter an expletive. They always sounded funnier in Arabic, so we'd laugh again.

It's subtle, but you may have noticed that my maternal grandmother and my paternal grandfather came from the same house, making my mother and father distant cousins.

This explains nothing about my family.

How We Got Here

"On a boat" is the obvious answer. Aha! But not the same boat.

On my father's side, my great-grandmother was the first to emigrate. She was an entrepreneur, peddling sundries from house to house. When she had raised enough money, she sent, not for her husband, but for Rashid, her oldest son, my father's father. When you think about it, this made perfect sense. It was an early example of feminist activism and an innovative childcare initiative.

Leveraging their accumulated wealth into two peddler's outfits, Great-Grandma and Grampa Rashid worked to raise the money to bring the rest of the family to the U.S. When they had enough, Rashid set out to get them. Fearing that any money sent back to the old country would be lost in the breakup of the crumbling Ottoman Empire, my grandfather had a brainstorm. He purchased cases of Winchester rifles, took them back to Lebanon and sold them there. Thus, before the age of majority, my grandfather had developed two careers, peddler and gunrunner, and there were more to come.

He married his betrothed, Mariana, while back in Lebanon. Before he could take her back to America, he had to build her a house. (Hey! I didn't write this story; I'm simply telling it.)

Rashid eventually brought his wife, his father, his sister Salima, and his brother Habib back to America, leaving behind his youngest brother for unexplained reasons.

The Proof of the Pudding

Several years ago I happened to be traveling in France. Upon returning to my hotel one day, I heard the concierge speaking what was obviously a Lebanese dialect of Arabic. I approached him and greeted him in the same dialect. He stared briefly and responded, "I thought you were an American."

"I am, but my great-grandparents were from Lebanon."

And then he said it. He actually asked, "What house are you from?"

"The house of Zennie," I replied.

He looked at me and asked, "Do you know the story of your family?" That's when I knew I was in big trouble. I was going to have to apologize to somebody. He proceeded to tell me the story of King Richard's lieutenant, the village headman, the daughter, etc., etc. He even added extra detail, placing the knight's geographic origin in what seemed to be the Tyrol region.

I was standing there, nonplussed and flabbergasted, when he asked, "Do you know Edmund Zennie?" (The first name was pronounced something like Ud-moon, with equal stress on both syllables.)

I replied, "Yes."

What happened from this point on is predicated on the popularity of Edmund Zennie. Cousin Edmund was a world-champion wrestler in a time period, and in a geographical area, when and where that meant something. On several occasions, he came to the U.S. to visit my grandmother — his cousin — in Dayton, Ohio.

Four-year-old that I was the first time I saw him, I recall him being about nine feet tall. From his shoulder, where he perched me, I could see his cauliflower ear. He spoke in an odd manner, which I later realized was attributable to deafness, not his Lebanese accent.

I filled in the concierge on these details of my childhood, and his level of excitement increased. He began making phone calls and jabbering in Arabic at a pace too quick for me to follow. I caught the occasional "Zennie" and "American," but that didn't provide much insight.

Later that evening, however, the mystery explained itself when I got a call from the concierge summoning me to the lobby. He had gathered what seemed like the entire Arabic émigré population of Western Europe into the ballroom, and a party had begun. While not quite the "guest of honor," that distinction being reserved for the spirit of Cousin Edmund, I nevertheless basked in the wrestler's reflected glory for several hours.

Waking up the next morning to check out, I held my breath for fear that the entire gala had been charged to my VISA card, but I should have had more faith in Lebanese hospitality.

On my next visit to the cemetery (in any Mediterranean culture these visits happen frequently), I apologized to my grandfather.

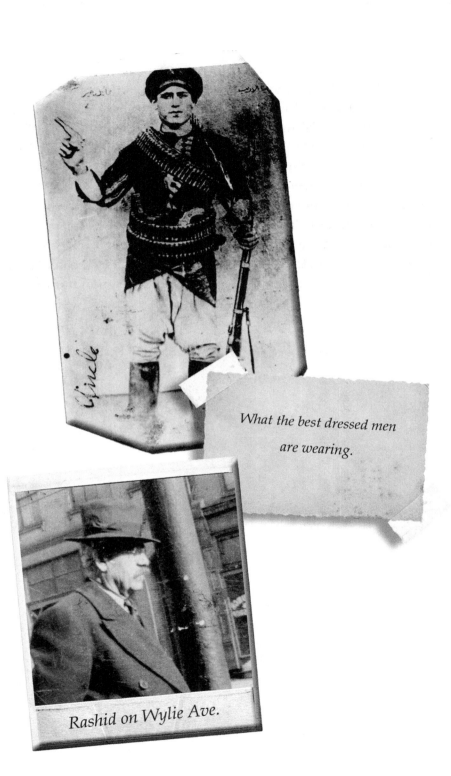

What the best dressed men
are wearing.

Rashid on Wylie Ave.

Wedding Day for Joseph and Betrosea. (His mother Jamila serves as Matron of Honor.)

Chapter Three

Before the Igloo

I ronically, in the late stages of one of the most recent Penguin runs to the Stanley Cup, my fondest memories of Mellon Arena, the Igloo, were about when it wasn't there. For most of my preteen life, I lived where the Mellon Arena once stood, in a large house with a large extended family at 1007 Wylie Avenue. Living in a large house with a large extended family was the rule rather than the exception in the Lower Hill District. While I don't think it was a requirement, the primarily Mediterranean (that is the Italian, Greek, and Lebanese), as well as the African-American and Jewish populations, all seemed to adhere to this lifestyle choice.

I'm sure, in retrospect, that life in the Lower Hill couldn't possibly be as idyllic as I remember it; but even allowing for the romanticism of my childhood memories, life there was certainly rich and varied. Of course there were problems, but I have always regretted that, in all of the portraits of the period and the neighborhood, no one I have ever heard from has come close to capturing this richness, energy, and diversity.

If we didn't like what we had for dinner, we simply stopped by the Paonessa's to dine Italian; and we naturally returned the favor. The Middle Eastern dishes my aunt and mother turned out — many of them meatless — were especially welcome among my friends on Fridays. The impossibly rich pastries at Caputo's coffee shop "down Wylie Avenue," Tambellini's on the corner, lemon ice at Pete Sacco's, fried baloney sandwiches at Joe Abraham's, and several neighborhood stores and delicatessens rounded out the culinary possibilities.

For recreation, there were baseball and softball at the sandlot on Washington Street, or hoops and boxing at the Pittsburgh Catholic Lyceum. Owned by Epiphany Church, the Lyceum was open to almost anyone. It was also the training home for many boxers of the era — for example Charlie Affif, Fritzie Zivic, Billy Conn, and world champion Harry Greb. Washington Park "up by Connelly Trade School" was home to several football leagues. Of course, any stoop or building could be transmogrified into an athletic venue with a simple rubber ball.

Elementary education took place at St. Peter's on Fernando Street (if you were Italian) or at Epiphany on Washington Street if you were Irish. We heard about some kids who attended a public school called "Forbes," but that was beyond our experience. To us "Forbes" was a street (not even an "Avenue"). For some reason, most of the Lebanese families (who were Maronite Catholic) sent their children to the Irish parish, rather than to the Italian one where they would have looked pretty much like everyone else. As a Lebanese kid at an Irish parish, I spent my childhood praying for freckles.

Now, don't get me wrong. This was not Camelot. Racial issues occasionally heated up, and I know that many of my black friends and acquaintances experienced the Lower Hill much differently. But I did have black friends, and some of them did attend school with me at Epiphany. (Many of their families frequented my father's tavern in the Uptown district. For half a century he dispensed wisdom with the beer and often a helping hand with the rent.) Some of the differences they told me about later on shamed me. In the early 50s we began to hear rumors about "redevelopment" and "renaissance." And most of us knew that the benefits wouldn't apply to us. Michael Weber provided the clearest explanation I have ever seen of the divergence in attitudes about Pittsburgh's first Renaissance in his excellent Davey Lawrence biography, Don't Call Me Boss. As I recall the explanation, Weber maintains that the city fathers were pleased because they paid the owners the market value for their homes. The denizens of the Lower Hill were angry because the market value often wasn't enough to purchase a home elsewhere. Of course, the impact of "redeveloping" people out of a business was another issue.

By the early sixties, the Civic Arena rose gleaming over the patch of ground where my house once stood. By this time I was attending Central Catholic High School, and I recall participating in a writing contest to celebrate the opening of the Arena. The contest asked students to compare the domes of the world (for example, St. Peter's, and so on) to the arena. I somehow couldn't drum up much enthusiasm for the project.

So please pardon me if, while I reveled in the latest Penguin run-up to Lord Stanley's Cup, I can't fully embrace the Igloo as all things good.

Chapter Four

Christmas Tide

G rowing up, Christmas was my favorite time of year. With so many kids, and parents who appreciated them, Christmas at the Kail home was a special blessing.

Much of the celebration was religious in nature. It is a definite understatement to say that the family was active in the parish. We lived two short blocks from Epiphany Church, and it was often the center of our social as well as our religious life. We were in the choir and served as altar boys. If you had a bingo night, you got the Kail kids to set up, call the bingo numbers, serve the food, take down, and clean up. If the priest was driving some of the women home from the Legion of Mary meeting, call one of the Kail kids to ride along and avoid scandal.

Our church celebrated a Mass at 2:30 a.m. on Sundays, Christmas, and New Year's. It was a relic of the days when Pittsburgh had seven or eight newspapers. It was the hour when the newspaper people finished the early edition, and was called the Printers Mass for many years. For close to thirty of those years, one or the other of my brothers or I would serve that Mass every week, as well as on Christmas and New Year's.

At Christmas, the involvement intensified. Eventually, the schedule for the oldest three boys on Christmas day included serving or singing at Midnight Mass, serving the 2:30 Mass, serving the Mass at Dawn, and serving or singing at the Solemn High Mass at 11 on Christmas morning. Obviously, the child labor laws were not applicable.

Eventually, I was the only one of the boys left at home, and I was still serving 2:30 Mass. I would sometimes bring my friends with me to Mass rather than cut off the evening early. After Mass I might bring them to the house for a breakfast of coffee or tea with pound cake and other pastries (see story "Pound Cake and Nut horns"). But not on Christmas.

On Christmas morning, the house rules stated that the kids couldn't approach the Christmas tree and the gifts unless adults were present. On Christmas morning, I developed the habit of eating breakfast after Mass and then dozing in the living room by the tree until the younger kids got up, so that I could watch them open their gifts.

At about 5:30 or 6 a.m. you would begin to hear them, like mice, scrabbling along the hall, gathering at the top of the stairs, Patty and Theresa whispering loudly, wondering if it was time to go down. I could hear the whispers. "What time is it?" "Is there a grownup down there?" "I don't know; is Eugene a grown-up?"

Luckily, before anyone would have to answer that last question, their "whispers" would have wakened the rest of the house, and they could run down the stairs, burst into the living room around the tree, and open their gifts. Another house rule required you to open gifts one at a time, placing the wrappings in the strategically placed plastic garbage bag.

By the time I was twelve or thirteen, I had begun making enough from selling papers and odd jobs that I could afford to buy simple presents for everyone in the family. I took pride in selecting just the right present for each member of the family, even though it might be small or inexpensive. It was easy to bask in the illusion that mine was everyone's favorite gift.

This was an attitude I shared with my Aunt Philomena, who was mentally challenged. She was unquestionably the most loving and most innocent person I have ever known, and she had a monopoly on the easiest simple gifts. In one short shopping trip, with one or two of the family who were sworn to secrecy, she would corner the market on handkerchiefs, shoe shiners, combs, playing cards, change purses, and so on, leaving me to exert more imagination or more muscle power to come up with my gifts.

Our tradition was to decorate the tree on Christmas Eve. It seemed like we had hundreds of bulbs. And then there was the annual Yuletide argument about whether to use the foil icicles or "angel hair," the spun glass that was so difficult to handle. Inevitably, the icicles would win out, and then Uncle Joe would remind everyone to place them on the tree from the inner branches out, and then remind us several times again. Of course, the best decorations were the piles of wrapped packages in all colors stacked under the tree.

We had eight- or ten-foot ceilings, so the tree was usually at least seven feet tall. Interestingly, we seldom decorated outside, except to place a wreath on the door.

The fragrance of food always permeated the house, tomato sauce or an Arabic dish, often with a heavy but pleasant underlay of garlic. At Christmas, however, the house was dominated by smells of baking — sugar, cinnamon and butter — as Aunt Martha or Grandma would make the Middle-Eastern pastry called baklawa, layers of filo dough stuffed with walnuts, suffused with sugar syrup and possibly rose water, and then baked.

Eventually, it became the tradition for the girls — i.e., the six daughters of the house — to do most of the Christmas baking, and even to take over the preparation of some of the Arabic dinner elements. Given the level of quality established by Aunt Martha, Mom and Grandma, God forgive me, but I have to admit that the results were often hit or miss. Except for Rosanne's cookies. She turned out a variety, ranging from the standard chocolate chip and peanut butter, to a "sandwich" of sugar cookies on either side of some type of jam. I always managed to smuggle home a few leftover cookies. (I may never get another chance at leftovers if the girls see this qualified praise.)

When we were younger, and still living on Wylie Avenue, we actually had three trees on a triple platform, with a pretty extensive model train set wending its way around them. One of the highlights of the season was the single dollar bill that old Mrs. Jacob, a family friend, would pin to the tree for each of us.

As we got older, new traditions developed. Every year I would hold a Christmas Brunch on the Saturday before Christmas. Dick would invite everyone over on the afternoon of Christmas Eve, and Bob would host a Christmas Eve gathering that night. I often left early from Bob's, since I was still, for many years, cantoring at Midnight Mass and serving the 2:30 Mass.

Every year Dick would find an opportunity to remind us of our choral roots. He, Bob, and I would end up singing the carols we had sung as choirboys many years before. For just a few moments, it would become quiet enough to hear us sing, in two- or three-part harmony, the old Latin hymns that meant Christmas to us as kids: "Quem Pastores" and "Adeste Fideles."

Nowadays, Christmas dinner is served buffet style, and everyone pitches in. (Ask Franny or Judy about that last statement. and they'll laugh and call me a liar to my face.) In the years before grandchildren, however, it was still a sit-down feast. Since the bar was closed, my mother and father were home, so both Mom and Aunt Martha would cook.

The menu was likely to consist of a turkey (at least 20-25 lbs.), and a large ham, along with some kibbee. (This is the Lebanese national dish, consisting of beef or spring lamb, pulverized in a large marble receptacle to remove the fat and gristle, mixed with bulgur wheat, green peppers, onions, mint, cumin, and a number of other herbs and spices, and served raw.)

Then we would add incidentals like rice with pine nuts, green beans in tomato sauce, a tossed salad, cranberry sauce, and a variety of other sides that happened to be in fashion at the moment. Years later, as Mariann and her daughter Casondra became vegetarians and then vegans, more vegetable dishes would be added, and tofu began to play a part on the menu (but not a large one).

Christmas in the Kail household always lasted the full twelve days from December 25 to January 6, the feast of the Epiphany, sometimes called "Little Christmas." In Lebanese families, the Epiphany was celebrated with zlabia, a fried pastry with anise that was dipped in syrup before eating.

We had a further reason for the holiday. It was the feast of our parish, the Church of the Epiphany, and we would commemorate it with what were then called "Forty Hour" services. The ceremonies had an opening and a closing, and included hymns, processions, prayers, and multiple priests. To a young kid in a cassock and a surplice, the services often seemed to last the full forty hours.

As with Christmas, New Year's Eve was celebrated with a 2:30

a.m. Mass.

A bizarre telephone process would develop at certain times during the year when we celebrated 2:30 Mass — for example, when we would change from Daylight Savings Time to Eastern Standard Time, and back again. Unlike Christmas, however, the loony factor expanded. This is the loony process: An amazing number of people would phone the parish rectory to inquire, "Will there be a 2:30 Mass this morning?" "Yes, there will be."

"What time will it be?" (Thus the loony factor.)

One of the Kail boys would inevitably be called on to answer phones at the rectory until about 2 a.m. when he would leave to prepare for 2:30 Mass.

By the time January 6 arrived, although we would never admit it, we were ready to get back to school.

Mom and Dad celebrate Christmas (at Bob's)

Bob and me with Santa

34

Chapter Five

Grade School Days

E piphany School on Washington Street, like the parish of which it was a part, was heavily Irish, with everything that implied in 1950s America, both positive and negative. Like many schools filled with the children of the immigrant working class, Epiphany had a strong representation among those who would go on to high school, and even college, and eventually success (depending on how you defined it).

St. Peter School and Parish stood one block over on Fernando Street, and were home to most of the Italian population of the Hill District. A few blocks further up the Hill was Holy Trinity, which eventually became St. Benedict the Moor. Years ago it had been primarily German, but in the seventies it became primarily African-American. Further up the Hill was St. Anne, the Maronite Catholic Church; it had no school attached.

The vast majority of the Lebanese families in the Hill District were Maronite Catholic. Wanting a Catholic education for their kids, they sent their children to the Irish parish rather than to the Italian one. They were simply doing what every wave of immigrants had done before them. They were social climbing. Essentially, they felt that the Irish were "more American" than the Italians.

By the time I attended, a large portion of the student body was comprised of those who would eventually drop out and enter the large proportion of Pittsburgh's population who did physical labor. Or maybe they would enter the rackets. (When it came to crime, Pittsburgh was purportedly an "open city," meaning that none of the major crime families controlled it — although several had some representation. And Lena Horn maintained in a 1980s Dick Cavett interview that her father "controlled much of the numbers business in Pittsburgh.")

Much of the lower Hill District was already abandoned; its streets lined with empty houses, piles of rubble, and closed businesses. Out of the thirty or forty pupils in my eighth grade, there seemed to be as many students who were arrested as went on to high school. Yet, as best I can figure, eight or ten attended college (not a bad percentage for the time, now that I think about it).

As with their parish life, the Kail kids became extremely active in the life of the school. From CYO dances to spelling bees, from schoolyard games to leaning against the wall looking cool, one or more of the Kails not only participated, they were likely to have set it up, or would be in charge of cleaning up afterwards — except the "looking cool" part.

After we moved from Wylie Avenue in the Hill to Fifth Avenue, in what was usually called Oakland, I was the only one who remained in the Hill at Epiphany School. My older brothers had graduated. Everyone below me in age transferred to St. Agnes School, across the street from our new home.

I would take the public bus to school each morning, and take it home again at night. In those days, few schools had a cafeteria. Most students were still likely to walk home for lunch. Since time and distance made it impractical for me to do so, I typically walked four blocks to the family bar, got money from my mother to buy lunch somewhere along Fifth Avenue — most often at the lunch counter at Darling's Drug Store — and usually returned to the bar to eat it.

I'm sure this did immeasurable emotional and social damage, but I actually enjoyed it. If my mother weren't free, one of the regulars would inevitably shelter me from whatever I shouldn't see.

The Mercy Nuns taught us at both Epiphany and St. Agnes, so we got to know them pretty well. They were heavily "lace curtain" Irish, as opposed to someone like the Sisters of Charity, who were likely to have a strong strain of "Shanty Irish." The "Mercies" even had a plate warmer in the kitchen.

Most of them were a bit autocratic, but they had an excellent sense of humor. And even though it sometimes took a while for them to warm up to us swarthy Lebanese, many of them, such as Sister Rosina and Sister Madeline, became our good friends. While in high school and college, I would often return to substitute in the classroom.

My brother Bob received a grant to complete part of his college education in return for teaching full time at Epiphany. With his red Vespa motor scooter, blue eyes and dark complexion, he naturally became the darling of the grade-school set.

Aside from Sister Rosina, my favorite nun was Sister Bonaventure, the principal during my later years. She had grown up to her full four-feet-ten-inches in a small Pennsylvania oil town, in a large family with lots of brothers. Far from being "lace curtain," she was a tough old broad, and we got along well. We often shared family stories, and she was one of the few nuns who could beat me at poker.

Unfortunately, she was in her late seventies or early eighties and would occasionally "lose it." Whether from Alzheimer's or simple dementia, she would often forget things or lose the thread in the middle of a conversation. Only once did this really cause a problem for me.

One lunchtime, Sister Bonaventure told me to stay outside on traffic patrol for a while longer to help some late students get across the street. This would make me late for class, but wasn't much out of the ordinary. Only, this time, she forgot. When I reported late for class, she happened to be outside the eighth-grade door and began questioning my tardiness.

I should have simply said "sorry" and ended the controversy. But I was a young adolescent, which meant I was stupid. I was also arrogant and egotistical, with a strong streak of self-righteousness, and I wouldn't let it go. We got into a shouting match and, eventually, she told me I was suspended.

I huffed and puffed, packed up my books, and headed for the bar to inform my mother of this glaring injustice. She was curiously unresponsive. She sat me down on the corner barstool and left me to contemplate my status. An occasional regular would stop by to say hello and express solidarity with the oppressed, but that's all the sympathy I got. By this time, I realized I was in trouble.

The next morning, in her typically even-tempered way, my mother accompanied me on the bus, walked with me to the school, matter-of-factly waited until the opening activities were completed, and then walked me to the principal's office, where she made me apologize for the disrespect I showed.

To this day, I have so much respect for my mother. She didn't take sides with the established powers, defend her innocent son, or waste time trying to establish the "real" facts of the situation. She didn't try to assess blame or make me admit I was wrong. She just made me apologize for the disrespect.

Sister Bonaventure simply smiled and sent me to class. I'm sure she didn't remember the earth-shattering controversy of the day before. I sometimes use this "suspension" story when I make presentations to educational audiences. My policy is full disclosure.

• • •

They really didn't know what to do with me at Epiphany School, so they took the expedient approach, and gave me a great deal of unstructured time — almost an independent-study curriculum — which they then proceeded to fill with a series of questionable tasks.

On Monday I would be released to deposit the results of the Sunday collection at the local bank. I was a thirteen-year-old kid carrying several thousand dollars through the toughest neighborhood in the city. But I was one of the Kail kids, so it must be OK.

On Tuesday I would teach the younger altar boys how to serve Mass and Benediction.

On Wednesday I would carry money downtown to the Port Authority to purchase bus passes for those students who wanted them.

On Thursday or Friday I would often assist Sister Madeline with the special-education class.

I frequently went shopping for the sisters. That is, I would be sent with money or a charge card to purchase things for them, since they were usually unable to do these things for themselves. There seemed to be a whole unofficial-but-nevertheless-effective network of workers at the Downtown department stores who, at a phone call from one of the sisters, acted like a Sears catalogue. Essentially, they would prepare the purchase, and I would deliver it. I spent hours wandering around Kaufmann's or Gimbel's or Rosenbaum's or Frank & Seder's, the Downtown department stores.

I, of course, would conscientiously spend as much time as was necessary to complete the tasks — sometimes even stopping to eat at a Downtown diner to keep my strength up. Occasionally in need of a rest after walking into town, I might have to stop at a movie theater to find a place to sit down for a while.

• • •

As he grew older, our pastor, Father O'Connell, became progressively more deaf. This wasn't particularly burdensome to the students until First Friday came along, when the school required us to go to Confession on Thursday afternoon, and attend Mass on Friday. The whole school would line up, grade by grade, and march over to the church where three or four priests would be waiting in the confessionals, anxious to shrive us.

Then the jostling would begin. As you progressed down the line, you would carefully count the number of students in front of you, divide them by the number of priests available and then factor in the RSOC (relative speed of confession), to determine the likelihood that you would end up with Father O'Connell. Then, if necessary, you would begin evasive action. You might step out of line to ask Sister a question and step back in a safer position. Or you might ask permission to go to the boy's room with the same ending maneuver. (Once more than a few people learned these techniques, however, the traffic pattern became more complex than an airport, with significantly less safety.)

You never wanted to end up in Father O'Connell's confessional, because you would have to shout to be heard. And "heard" involved the whole church and the entire enrollment of the school, the "man in the street" (and most of the women as well), and the occupants of any passing car.

"You did what? I can't hear you."

(Almost shouted) "I HARBORED IMPURE THOUGHTS!"

You prayed fervently for invisibility upon exiting the confessional.

39

Maybe they wouldn't know who was in there.

By the time we graduated from Epiphany, we were ready for the challenge of Central Catholic High School.

Miss Brady's fourth grade class recites an opening prayer.

Chapter Six

The Family Bar

My father dropped out of the University of Pittsburgh to take care of his brother and two sisters. His father had become pretty much a recluse after the death of his wife at a very young age. The extensive real estate holdings Rashid had acquired over the years, he lost to delinquent taxes.

Before the war, my dad's first real job was with his Uncle Habib, who had developed a series of Downtown parking lots. They were forced out of the parking-lot game by the Big Players. Family legend maintains that the "Big Players" were "connected."

This proved to be a temporary setback. Somehow Habib must have found new parking territory to exploit. His sons, grandsons and even great-grandsons remained in the business and currently run/own several lots.

During World War II, my father got a job as a machinist at Mesta Machine Works and worked his way up to foreman. Then he became ill and was bed-ridden for almost a year. After the war, in 1946, my maternal grandfather, Joe, helped Dad and Grampa Rashid to open a grocery store at 101 Logan Street in the lower Hill District.

Finally, in 1948, Dad joined with an old friend to open a bar, Sokol and Kail's (thus "the S&K"), on Fifth Avenue in Uptown. At first, they served a mixed clientele: white, black, and even a significant number of Latinos. There was not yet a large Mexican migration heading north to Pittsburgh, but what population existed was drinking at "Dave's place." Wonderful murals of Mexico and the Latino population graced the walls thanks to my cousin Henry Samreny. The S&K remained there until the area was "redeveloped" in the early sixties. For some inexplicable reason, the redevelopers felt it was imperative to extend McGee Street, which ended at Fifth Avenue, all the way up to Colwell Street, a distance of one block. The S&K was in the way.

Since they were renters at the original site of the S&K, Dad and his partner received a munificent $200 for the move. Even with 1960 buying power, $200 didn't go a long way. Interestingly, within a year or two, the site they had vacated to create a through street was blocked off at both ends and turned into a parking lot. (Does somebody sense a theme here?)

My father was forced to develop a new facility two blocks up Fifth Avenue, in an old furniture store, incurring major debt. In that space, they would eventually become the A.H.P. My dad said that the letters stood for some new partners. My mother decided they meant "A Happy Place."

By this point in the Pittsburgh Renaissance, my father had been "redeveloped" out of some parking lots, out of the grocery business, and out of a tavern. Refusing to declare bankruptcy, he insisted on paying off all of his debts; it took years. I don't think he was out of debt until he was in his seventies.

• • •

The bar — and at this stage it was definitely a bar, not a tavern — really was a special place, as my mother always maintained. It served as a sort of safety zone. It had a diverse collection of regulars, more than 70% African-American, who became like an extended family. My mom and dad, each often unknown to the other, frequently lent money to the regulars, and got more than a couple of them out of a jam. This was not a patronizing relationship; Dad genuinely liked his customers, and often chose his friends from among them. For instance he and Arthur Giles were close for years. At Arthur's death, my father wept. I had never seen him do that before.

After working a six-day week, Dad would again head for the bar on Sunday evening after dinner, maintaining the fiction that he was setting up for Monday morning. We all knew he was meeting his buddies, probably to play cards. At his funeral, among Dad's pallbearers were his favorite cop, his favorite bartender, and his favorite bookie, all Sunday night regulars.

Unlike other businesses where clients come and go, at the A.H.P.

they just came. Only death forced them to "go." Even if they left Pittsburgh, they were sure to return to "Dave and Helen's place" when they stopped back in town.

There were some other notable "regulars," and they deserve a book of their own, although no one will ever write it. They include characters like Ted the Bartender (who became a member of the family), Don the baker (who baked wonderful cheesecakes), Tilly (who became Mom's best friend), Bishop McDowell who would send his embarrassed secretary, Mildred, to pick up appropriate beverages when he entertained), and also Black Beauty (who was).

Money was frequently scarce. My parents, and, therefore, the family, sometimes lived hand to mouth (the hand contained food). They went through periods when there wasn't a penny to spare, except for the church and for the bookie. At these times, they would use the cash register like a purse or wallet, with great faith that it would balance, somehow, at quarterly tax time. My parents were steadfast in their faith.

As they aged, and the severe arthritis that afflicted both of them gradually worsened, my mother and father became more of a "presence" than full time bar managers.

When my dad was killed as the result of a traffic accident in 1987, my mother was fearful that she wouldn't be able to take over total management of the bar. We all knew that she was much the better businessperson, and would do fine.

For years after my father's death, bar patrons would approach my mother with cash in their hands, wanting to be sure to pay back the money that Dave had lent them, however many months or years ago. Mom managed the bar on her own for another ten years.

• • •

Once, while my mother was still running the bar, which is the same as saying "while she was still alive," I was asked to consult for a PBS documentary called "Wylie Avenue Days." Until our move to Soho in the late fifties, we lived at 1007 Wylie Avenue. The documentary was attempting to capture what life was like in the neighborhoods

43

bordering this historic street that bisected Pittsburgh's Hill District. Chris Moore from WQED-TV produced it.

Over and over again Chris, who happened to be black, heard stories of "Dave and Helen's," or the old S&K. He asked to set up an interview on videotape with my mother that was supposed to last for ten minutes. It ended up taking almost a full hour.

The day before, at the house, I had picked out one of Mom's dresses and said, "You should wear this tomorrow. It will come over well on TV."

"What TV?"

"Tomorrow's interview."

"I'm not going on no TV. I thought he was interviewing me with a pencil and paper."

She finally agreed to do a TV interview, but insisted that I go into the bar before they began shooting to warn everybody. I entered and shouted, "If any of you told your wife or boss that you were somewhere else, you might want to finish your drink and leave for a while." Several regulars stood up and departed.

Chris was particularly fascinated by stories of the riots that took place after the Martin Luther King assassination in 1968, and questioned my mother closely.

The story she told began with a phone call in late afternoon from a friend who told her to lock up and go home. "They're moving down the Avenue, and they'll be at the bar pretty soon. Don't worry, we'll take care of your place."

My mother sent her customers home and had the porter place the barstools on the bar to facilitate mopping the floor. She then turned out the lights and was about to lock the door and leave, when the door burst inward and a group of mostly teens and young black men burst in and knocked a few stools onto the floor.

Turning to face them, my mother calmly told them there was no reason for them to be there, and they could just leave. Some of them, recognizing "Miss Helen," sheepishly turned and began to slip away.

She followed up with, "And there's no reason for those stools to be on the floor."

"What did they do then?" asked Chris.

"They picked them up."

Not a single window in the bar's Georgian front was damaged.

My parents were good people; they were not saints. Yet, they were accepting of everyone; they truly judged people "by the content of their character."

If there is a Kail family legacy, that ranks high as part of it.)

• • •

At my father's death, the large St. Agnes Church was almost filled for the funeral, half by family and friends, and half by the regulars from the bar, family and friends as well.

When my mother passed away, we briefly discussed opening a high-concept restaurant in the bar space, since we all liked to cook. Very briefly. It took us only a few minutes to remember the exhausting work my parents had done for a half-century.

We held on to the bar for several years. We wanted to find a buyer who understood, and would preserve, its role in the neighborhood and community. We had several nibbles, but kept losing money as we waited for just the right person.

Finally, a gentleman who owned a small grocery store in the area made an offer. We considered him the ideal candidate, and worked to solidify his financing, until we finally signed it over to him. We were very proud that we had been able to preserve a bit of our family heritage.

Within a year, he had turned it into a strip joint, it had been declared a nuisance bar, and he'd had his license suspended.

At least we tried.

Dad in typical pose at the family bar

Dick, Bob, Mike and I
in front of
1007 Wylie Avenue.

Chapter Seven

Hannah the Witch

E very kid in the neighborhood hated old Hannah the Witch. Please understand; none of us had ever met old Hannah the Witch. We might perhaps have seen her once or twice, from a distance, sweeping the sidewalk in front of the God Is Love Church on the corner of Wylie Avenue and Congress Street.

You see, Hannah made our balls disappear. This was possible because the church's six- or seven-foot gray wooden fence closed off one end of the back alley where we played baseball. Ours was an esoteric version of America's pastime, defined by the topography of the playing field.

A dumping area for the detritus from a galvanizing plant stretched along a small gully on the left side. The EPA would have been horrified, if it had existed then. You couldn't really chase a ball down the gully into the foul smelling iron receptacles. You'd likely break a leg or scratch something and die of blood poisoning. A ball hit into "the dump," as we called it, was either one out or three outs, depending on the rules of the day and how many balls we had.

A couple of fenced-in backyards formed the border on the right side of the field. A ball landing in the Paonessas' or the Nicholases' yard constituted a ground-rule double — or sometimes an out. It depended. In the narrow confines of that back alley, a ten- or twelve-foot-wide swath of furiously contested turf, we trained ourselves to hit screaming line drives that could take off your head if not handled dexterously by a glove man.

The adventure was compounded by the composition of the ground. There was no concrete, grass, or asphalt. You might occasionally see some broken cement buried beneath the dirt, but the predominant surface consisted of "red dog," plus broken glass, bottle caps, ancient newspapers, wood shavings, an occasional nail, and what passed for gravel and dirt. You tended to avoid sliding into second to break up a double play.

Unlike almost any other baseball venue in the land, if any of those line drives sailed over the fence that closed off the far end of the alley, instead of the home run indicated by tradition, it constituted an automatic forfeit by the offending batter's team.

For the same reason, our version of alley football contained no punts or field goals.

The problem was Hannah the Witch. Any ball hit over that fence was lost. She would make it disappear. Not that we would ever see her exercising her black arts, but we would never see those balls again either. At least that's what we told each other, usually in a whisper.

I met Hannah a few years later. She had stopped in front of our house to speak with my mother, smiled at me kindly, and performed not one feat of black magic. If she were a witch, why didn't she cure the crippling arthritis that disfigured her hands? What agony it must have been for her to be out sweeping the sidewalk each day.

Turns out she had no knowledge of our lost balls. She never ventured into the backyard except to hang clothes in a corner portion. The balls are probably still there, rotting, or more likely buried under the concrete floor of the Civic Arena — or the parking lot that replaced it.

Luckily, this youthful scapegoating didn't carry over into our relationships with the rest of our neighbors. Actually, we got along very well. The Paonessas lived three doors up, and they had a child cognate for almost every one of ours: Dick and Frank, Bob and Junior, Jimmy and I, and so on with the daughters.

What was more important, Mama Sarah was a superb Italian cook, and we were always welcome at her table. Oddly, her meatballs were slightly crisp or crunchy and relatively small. They were not cooked in sauce, but the flavor was memorable (obviously). It's hard to describe them on paper, but they provide the standard by which those of us who grew up in that section of the Hill District judge meatballs. At last count, no one had yet matched the quality.

The Paonessa kids were equally welcome at our house, where they often took advantage of our Lebanese meatless cuisine on Fridays, far superior to the tuna-noodle casserole or the Mrs. Paul's Frozen Fried Fish Sticks they were likely to be served at home.

We liked the Paonessas so much that we didn't mind when, for a few weeks each autumn, truckloads of grapes would block the alley, followed by a torrent of foul-smelling liquid that would flood our "ball field" and flow down the alley toward the sewer. We knew that this wastewater from the wine-making process would eventually lead to barrels of wine in the Paonessa basement, and a few bottles to bribe everyone along the alley.

The family on the right of us, facing the house, consisted of Nicky the Greek and his brother Ribsy (Bobby to his mother), notably skinny. (Notice that we defined the house by the children who lived there, not the family name.) Two houses to the left lived Skippy Scarpechio who was older and didn't loaf with us. Skippy lived with his mother Ruby. Nicky and Ribsy also lived with their family, but, since neither of the mothers approached the caliber of Sarah Paonessa as a cook, their impact on our lives was negligible. Immediately next door on the left lived Mrs. Johnson, a kindly black woman whose race is important only because it wasn't important.

At the second-floor level, several clotheslines on pulleys connected our two buildings, tenement fashion. Somewhere in the dim recesses of history we must have negotiated washdays, because I can never remember a conflict over the scheduling of their use.

Sometimes, I would see a young kid of my age named Danny Lloyd, who lived in the house, or else visited frequently. I never asked or cared which. I'm also not sure what his relationship was to Mrs. Johnson. He and I would explore the alley and its environs together, scaring the hell out of our respective caregivers, who readily imagined an infinite number of catastrophes that might befall us.

The blocks that formed our immediate neighborhood contained a drug store, a bar, a tailor, a bar, a baker, a barber, a bar, a butcher, a grocer, a bar, a bookie, a Cookie, a Felix, a Lisa, a Tensa, some Kails, some Johnsons, some Sianos, some Nassifs, some Catholic, some Assembly of God, and innumerable other elements that, as a rule, worked well together. What frictions that arose were smoothed over. While there were the typical childish stupidities, it took the bulldozers of redevelopment to tear that neighborhood apart. I miss it.

Chapter Eight

The Newspaper Stand

My family always maintained that the Lebanese "are middlemen, entrepreneurs, dealmakers."

"Beirut is the financial center of the Middle East," we were told. "We spring from the ancient Phoenician traders."

There's a joke that made the rounds a few years ago.

Lebanese Father: "It's time you got married. I have chosen a girl for you."

Son: "I will choose my own bride!"

Father: "But the girl is Bill Gates's daughter..."

Son: "Well, in that case ... OK."

Next, the Father approaches Bill Gates.

Father: "I have a husband for your daughter."

Bill Gates: "My daughter is too young to marry."

Father: "But this young man is a vice-president of the World Bank."

Bill Gates: "Ah, in that case... OK."

Finally, the Father goes to see the president of the World Bank.

Father: "I have a young man to recommend as a vice-president."

President: "I already have more vice-presidents than I need."

Farther: "But this young man is Bill Gates's son-in-law."

President: "Ah, in that case... OK."

And that's how the Lebanese do business.

I'm not sure if my brother Dick ever heard the joke, but it obviously characterized his business practices. When I was eleven or twelve, he bought a newspaper stand on the corner of Fifth Avenue and Diamond Street. "Buying a newspaper stand" meant more than purchasing a sort of metal table with shelves on which you placed the papers that were being stored or sold. And it was different from having a paper route, involving the right to deliver papers to subscribers in a particular area.

The heart of buying a stand was monopoly, the right to be the sole seller of newspapers in a particular area.

In the entrepreneurial spirit, Dick turned around and immediately made a deal with me, although I don't recall much negotiation. Every day after school, I would receive the paper delivery, set up the stand, and sell the papers. We would then split the profits. The deal worked well for several months.

(Our parents periodically experimented with "allowances," but a regular weekly handout of money never really caught on in the family. The newspaper stand represented a regular income — independence — for me.)

I don't really remember how long it lasted, but I know how it ended. One day I showed up at the stand to set up, and it was already occupied. I think the kid's name was Ralph, and he was a lot bigger than I was. I demanded my rights; he exercised his, and ultimately I ran home trying not to cry, expecting my big brother to defend our property.

"Oh, I forgot to tell you. I sold the stand to Ralphie," replied Dick, dispassionately, when I apprised him of the situation.

This was my introduction to the heartless world of business.

Later, Dick sort of atoned by getting me my own newspaper

stand that was even better. It was indoors at the Fisher Scientific factory.

And so my working life began.

With few exceptions, my employment history has been unorthodox at best. At sixteen I was a counselor at a fresh-air camp, and then I moved on to a summer camp for children with disabilities. I progressed to become an elevator operator and a professional bingo caller, served a stint at a Jewish day camp, and stayed on to serve as a social worker there. The highlight of my employment history was probably the two or three months I spent as choreographer at the Downtown Palace A-Go-Go. These latter jobs I did while I was coaching speech and debate at Central Catholic and performing onstage.

I was about to sign a contract to teach in the Pittsburgh Public Schools when my high-school debate coach, Brother Rene, informed me that I "owed" my alma mater a year. I actually spent twenty good years as a teacher at Central Catholic High School.

This diverse employment laid the basis for my eventual career at Eugene M. Kail & Associates, where the emphasis was on variety. Essentially, we undertook any task related to communications, education, and marketing. The connections I had made, and the experiences I'd had, provided me with the skills I needed to succeed for twenty years in my own business — or at least bluff well enough to get by.

I find it interesting, though, that, if you ask me what I do today, my first thought is always, "I'm a teacher."

There's one thing I have to admit, however: I have been either very blessed or very lucky, because for forty-some years, with few exceptions, I enjoyed getting up and going to work every day. I enjoyed what I did and those with whom I did it. There are, unfortunately, fewer and fewer people who can make a statement like that anymore. I was afraid there were none, but I was talking to an old friend, Jeff Muller, the other day; and he said he felt the same way. Since Jeff and his wife Amy are truly good people, I was idiotically happy for the rest of the day.

When word got around that I was opening my own business,

I was inundated with calls from friends and acquaintances who wanted to let me know they were available. Many of them added how much they hated their present job. The number of people who must hate to get out of bed in the morning, who spend most of their days, and most of their lives, hating what they do, struck me quite forcefully. They counted the minutes until retirement.

In my mind, "retirement" was just another word for opportunity. I never understood the concept of retiring to do nothing. I simply looked forward to doing the same things I enjoyed while working, only now I could do them for someone who needed the help but couldn't afford my fees.

While I was at Central, the pay scale was significantly less than the public-school scale. After I was forced to retire because of illness, the pension to which I was entitled for twenty-two years' work was almost ludicrous. But I never regretted for a moment the professional choices I made.

By this time, I had begun to wear glasses.

Chapter Nine

It's in the Cards

We very seldom had money in our family, so the traditional types of recreation were not usually available to us. We never ate in good restaurants, although we loved good diners. We seldom even went to a McDonald's or its equivalent. Olives, cheese, and Arabic bread constituted our fast-food menu. As far as I recall, we never stayed in a hotel or motel, and "vacation" consisted of driving to Dayton to visit my grandmother.

The individual social lives of the children were active. We discovered the Carnegie Library and Natural History Museum on our own, and spent hours there. We played sports, participated in parish life, and attended movies — often at the Fifth Avenue or the Rialto Theaters, where admission was a dime and you could see third-run films. Of course, we got into the standard types of mischief as well.

Most of our social life as a family, however, centered on people. Our house was always full of visitors who simply blended into the family. I don't know if it was a function of a lack of money, or the fact that my mother worked a six-day week, or simply happenstance, but our friends came to visit us. This was true of family as well. Aunt Gen and Uncle Rege were over several times a week. Cousin Mariann Habib, early on, would stop over for several hours when she was working a split shift. Cousins Henry and Tony were frequent visitors.

With the exception of stopping at the neighbors, we seldom ventured out socially. As time passed, Uncle Joe and Aunt Martha got abroad more frequently, but even their friends — men such as Bill Kulak and George Kudrav — spent a great deal of time at the house.

The only friend I can remember my mother visiting was Aunt Edith (an aunt through choice not blood). Edith and my mother had known each other since before their respective marriages. Edith, who was a bit older, had moved to Pittsburgh before my mother and then acted as a sort of sponsor or mentor when my mother later followed. She was a delightful woman, dignified, caring, with a wonderful sense of humor.

With so many people stopping by, the most frequent form of recreation was pretty basic, taking the form of good conversation and, of course, good food. From our earliest years, the children were included in the conversations, although we were strongly encouraged to have something to say before we said it.

A second major element of our family social life consisted of board games such as Monopoly or Scrabble, quiz games such as "Twenty Questions" or "Trivial Pursuit," and the like, and also card games.

In our family, "card games" meant poker, gin rummy, or 500 rum. There was a game of 500 going on in the dining room almost every night. The players would rotate as people would come or go. For some reason, Aunt Martha seemed to have a natural penchant for the game. She pretended to be cool about it, as if it didn't matter, but she was a shark.

On the other hand, my father, the unquestioned master of gin rummy, made no bones about it. He was delighted when he could nonchalantly drop the winning "Gin!" into the ongoing conversation. I could never understand it. He had a real card sense, knowing what was in my hand within a few tricks. Rumor had it that he even occasionally played for money at the bar with his friends, not that we would ever believe such a thing.

Uncle Joe would adopt the same attitude with Scrabble, taking great delight in drubbing you with an obscure word that netted a high point total.

And then there was poker — or, as we called it, "penny ante." The "penny" referred to the stakes when we played at the house. We usually played "five-card draw," or occasionally "seven-card stud." There was a set of house rules that was so complex you could have majored in it at college.

Some examples: It was always dealer's choice. The amount you could bet was limited. You could check and raise. You could bet out of turn. You could show your cards to someone to ask for help, and they couldn't bet against you. If you ran out of money, you could play "on poverty," and so on.

My favorite rule was the one my grandmother swore by; a wild card wasn't as good as a "natural" card. Thus, if you both had a ten-high straight, and one of your cards was a wild card, instead of splitting the pot, the person with the natural hand was the winner.

When the kids played, as we often did, wild cards proliferated. One young card shark called a game where the wild cards included "aces, deuces, treys, one-eyed jacks, king with the ax, queen, the card that follows, and low hole."

When I eventually began playing occasionally on the outside, I had to be careful I wasn't shot or knifed for reverting to house rules.

When we moved to Oakland in the late fifties, there was a stoop containing twelve or fifteen steps in front of our house. This constituted a front porch for the thousands of Pittsburghers forced to conform creatively to the urban landscape. On a warm evening, you would find anywhere up to fifteen or twenty people, of multiple genders and races, and a variety of ages, sitting two on a step.

The younger kids might be playing "handball" down on the sidewalk. This was not handball as you probably know it. This was more like tennis, with a tennis ball, your hand as a racquet, and a crack in the pavement as the "net."

The adult entertainment for the evening, for those sitting on the steps, might consist of "Twenty Questions," a game where the winner of each round had the opportunity to pose the next name or object — animal, vegetable, or mineral — to be uncovered in the allotted number of questions asked round robin.

Once, when I was still in my pre-teen days, a large group sat on the steps, engrossed in a game. I suddenly realized that the answer to the round we were playing was Nebuchadnezzar, the King of Babylon. We must have been studying him in school, because I have no idea why he popped into my head.

I waited for my turn to ask a question, praying that no one would get it before me. The games were very competitive, and a great deal of prestige was attached to stumping the audience or, conversely, to providing the right answer to an obscure question.

When my turn came, I proudly queried, "Is it Nuchakubundazar, King of Babylon?" For some reason, the two phrases were linked in my mind. I never said one without the other. As to the spelling given here, it is as close as I can get to what issued forth from my mouth in triumph. After all, I had read the name in a book; I had never heard it pronounced.

The laughter was immediate and raucous. "Who the hell is 'Nuchakubundazar'?" They wouldn't give an inch. Finally, I think it was either my cousin Henry or Bill Kulak who stood up for me and defended the answer. "He obviously means Nebuchadnezzar. Give him a break."

In all modesty, even from this viewpoint of a half-century later, I think it was a pretty impressive performance. How many ten- or twelve-year-olds would be able to identify this ancient potentate, even today? (If you have an answer to that question, remind yourself that it is strictly rhetorical.)

Up until a few years ago, however, if I ever paused to search for a word in the midst of a conversation, somebody was bound to holler out, "It's Nuchakubundazar!" and laugh like hell.

Bob sneaks up on an unsuspecting Gene, Mike and Mariann

Chapter Ten

The Church

We had a strange relationship with both the church and the Church. All four parents were devoutly religious. Raised as Maronite Catholics, they became Latin Rite in all but name, once their children started Catholic school at Epiphany (more elsewhere).

The Maronite Church was intertwined with the Lebanese culture, where it was born, and at various times became involved with Lebanese political life as well. But, in the fifties, the most obvious differences were liturgical.

The Latin Rite was the most familiar to Americans raised on movie priests like Bing Crosby and Barry Fitzgerald. It was difficult to confuse them with Middle-Easterners (although blonde, blue-eyed Gordon McRae did play a desert Arab leader in the movie musical Desert Song).

In the Latin Rite, most ceremonies had originally been conducted, logically enough, in Latin. The great liturgical composers we knew — men like Mozart, Bach, Palestrina, Rossini — tended to be German and Italian, but they wrote "church" music in Latin.

In the Maronite Rite, Aramaic was the liturgical tongue, "the language that Christ spoke," we were frequently reminded. They poured on the incense. Their garments, both daily and liturgical, came from different traditions, as did the music.

There were other differences, for instance, in sacramental theology. Latins maintained that the husband and wife administered the sacrament of Matrimony to each other, with the priest acting as a witness for the Church. The Maronites didn't beat around the bush. You could have a whole church full of witnesses, and, given the size of most Maronite families, you usually did; but the priest was there to administer the sacrament.

Our parents wanted us in a Catholic school, and their choice impacted more than our religious life. It had major implications for our social and cultural assimilation as well. Since we attended church as well as school at Epiphany, essentially, we lost a large part of our contact with the Maronite community. This was exacerbated when they redeveloped the Hill District. Almost all of the Maronite Catholic community moved south to Brookline and Dormont. We moved east to Soho/Oakland.

What we gained in this confusion of rites, however, tended to outweigh what we lost. We became close to both the parish and its priests. Since we lived only about two blocks away, the church called on us all of the time, and we were involved in everything. It sounds crazy, but the more we worked, the more we liked it. It made us feel that we belonged; we were on the inside.

Thus, the boys were progressively acolytes, choirboys, and altar boys. More than that, we were each, in turn, choir soloists, and masters of ceremonies. Whenever the church needed help, we were the first called.

In those days, the Sisters of Mercy who taught us were not permitted to be out at night; so, in order to get the altar boys, torchbearers, and choirboys into their cassocks, surplices, and various other accoutrements, mothers were drafted for evening services such as Midnight Mass, Forty Hours devotions, and the like. My mother and Mrs. Egan were among the stalwarts (although no one could ever explain Mrs. Egan, no one would ever challenge her either).

There were adventures implicit in being so close to the church. At least twice that I recall, when a lace surplice proved combustible, Father Basompierre found a new use for the cope, the large and heavily decorated cape the priest wears during Benediction. He simply flung it over the altar boy with the blazing surplice, in order to stifle the flames.

Sister Patricia Ann, the "altar boy nun," was old school and not used to being contradicted; so, when I refused to allow her to use Vaseline petroleum jelly to control my cowlick, I expected dire consequences. My mother, however, backed me rather than her. It was one of the high points of my altar-boy career.

By this time in that career, the duties of the Epiphany altar boys encompassed serving morning Mass at Epiphany (6:30 and 7; 7:30 and 8; or 6:30 Mass on the side altar), and also serving the Mass schedule at Mercy Hospital, Duquesne University, and the Allegheny County Jail, as well as at any hotels that were hosting a "Catholic" convention. They were all inside the borders of the parish. (We loved "hotel" duty. It usually involved missing your first class, a free breakfast, and an odyssey through Downtown Pittsburgh. As I have said elsewhere, since most of our friends were meeting similar commitments, we just assumed everyone was growing up this way.

My favorite assignments, though, were the times the priest would be baptizing a convert who had no Catholic friends to act as godparents. The pastor would simply call "one of the Kail kids." Since these were often joyous experiences, and were sometimes followed by a party or a dinner, we were happy to oblige.

Our social life was enhanced by hoops and boxing at the Pittsburgh Catholic Lyceum. Located across Washington Street from the church, it also had a large library. Owned by Epiphany, the Lyceum was open to the public and renowned (as I mentioned earlier) as the training place of champions.

A further connection was Camp O'Connell, the fresh-air camp situated on what was once Father O'Connell's family Farm. All of the older boys worked there at some point. We were still involved when Father O'Connell donated the land to the Variety Club to form a camp for children with disabilities. We worked several years under this arrangement as well.

In a time before it was considered standard practice, we developed individual friendships with the priests and nuns who ministered to us. Father Brennan, Father Kelly, Father DeCarlo, Father Henault, Father Groutt, they all knew the family well, sometimes stopped by, and often took several of us at a time on various adventures: to the amusement park, to visit a local farm, or to movies and theatres. (Father O'Connell was a good friend of J. P. Harris, developer of the first Nickelodeon and owner of the Ice Capades. The flow of free tickets from Harris to Father O'Connell to the Kail kids — and others — proved to be one of the perks of the relationship.)

Admittedly, it caused a bit of chagrin when six- or seven-year-old

Patty, having seen Father Ward remove his collar before attending the movies with us, reported to her homeroom nun that, "a priest was undressing at our house last night."

I can almost hear the snickers or see the frowns of disapproval. Let me make it clear: At no time in a long series of relationships with a large number of priests, brothers, and nuns, did any one of them make an inappropriate advance to me.

Instead, I recall wonderful moments and hilarious interactions. Father O'Connell, the founding pastor, was a wonderful man and priest, but was known to be a bit frugal. Occasionally, when the austerity became burdensome, one or another of his assistants would call one of the Kail boys for a food run. This might involve the purchase of a fried baloney sandwich from Joe Abraham's, or simply a box of Grape Nut Flakes, and a surreptitious delivery at the rear window of the rectory under cover of darkness.

And I recall trust. For example, on Mondays, one of us was likely to take the cash from the Sunday collections to deposit it at the bank. In retrospect, I find that amazing on any number of levels. I wouldn't trust me with that much money if the house were on fire.

Adulthood altered my theology and opinions a bit; age, as it should, has provided some perspective.

As I write this, I am looking at the cover of Time magazine; they just named Pope Francis as "Person of the Year." It's no wonder Francis has been received so well by the people; he has his priorities straight.

Now all he has to do is hold a Vatican auction, or maybe a house sale, to raise money to continue the service to people. I don't intend to get caught up in the "faith versus good works" controversy, but I'll take "faith plus good works" over the rulebook any time.

I can sum up my faith even more succinctly than my cynicism. To me, "the Church" means people more than canon law. And Christianity involves a life properly lived, motivated by a commitment to a set of beliefs, not simply a set of rules. It is the loving, not the legalities, that is of the essence.

Father Mike and friends

Chapter Eleven

Good Friday

T hinking back, I am amazed at the number of traditions that arose in the family, usually by accident. I guess most families develop traditions of one type or another; that's only logical, since most traditions are based on something that worked well, or made someone happy. We had, for instance, a whole collection of holiday traditions: how and when we decorated for Christmas, when we opened gifts, a sitdown dinner for Thanksgiving, a cookout for the fourth of July, and so on.

More and more in my memory, however, traditions were associated with holidays, and holidays were associated with church and food. This is not really surprising, since church and food permeated much of our lives. And not just Christmas and Thanksgiving. We even had traditions for Lent, Holy Week, and the Easter season.

For example, our church commitments were even more extensive at this time. It would begin with Ash Wednesday, the traditional start of Great Lent, as the Maronites called it. Of course, we would get ashes on our forehead to symbolize our mortality. That was a tradition shared by most of the Catholic Church. But we went further.

Each of us would choose something to give up for Lent. It had to be concrete and absolute. None of this "I will be nicer to people." It had to be something like "I will give up chocolate," or "I will give up comic books," or "I will give up gambling." And no "Monday, Wednesday, and Friday," like some of our wimpy friends. Furthermore, if the sacrifice we made for the season resulted in money being saved (e.g., from not buying gum or candy), we were supposed to give the saved money to the missions.

I'll never forget when I discovered in religion class that Sunday was not considered part of Lent. The Lord's Day was sacred in and of itself. This is why, for example, Catholics seldom had weddings on Sunday; it was already reserved to glorify God.

Wrapping myself in this analysis, a classic example of Jesuit casuistry if ever there was one, I knew there had to be an angle. Finally, I worked it out; and for two years running I gave up movies for Lent. Since we only went to the movies on Sunday, and Sundays were not part of lent, I was home free.

I forget who convinced me that it wasn't really likely that this approach conformed to the true spirit of Lent. It was probably a Christian Brother; they were no great admirers of the Jesuits. In any case, I went back to giving up candy the following year.

On the subject of candy, there were even traditions surrounding that. Dad loved nuts and chocolate, so each Easter, logically enough, we bought him a one- or two-pound chocolate egg with nuts — a Dimling"s one- or two-pound chocolate egg with nuts.

Another candy attitude concerned the sugar-covered, marshmallow chicks and rabbits available at this time of year. We preferred them stale. We loved the crunch and the superior chewability. It became a tradition. My mother and Aunt Martha became experts at taking the immense number of packages that we bought, and cutting a just-the-right-size slit that enabled them to go stale without spoiling. I think there was actually very little danger of spoilage, given their composition. I think they were made of sugar, coloring, and some substance with the half-life of plutonium.

It was also during Lent that we became poulterers, at least in a sense. In our neighborhood, it was a tradition to buy peeps during the Paschal season. I'm not sure what the origin of this activity was, since most people we knew bought baby rabbits, if they went in for livestock at all. But the habit was solidly fixed in our minds. Come Ash Wednesday, we went to the Five & Ten to buy peeps. If Woolworth's and Murphy's were selling them, I guess the practice was not really limited to our neighborhood.

Peeps, in case you didn't know, are baby chicks; and to add to the complexity of what we undertook, the peeps were often dyed in pastel colors. I have no idea whether there was a significance attached to the colors. Perhaps the whole activity was a holdover from our pagan past, and the peeps represented fertility or the coming of spring.

We would carefully feed and water these cute little birds, and change the paper in the box or bushel in which we kept them — for about a week. They were so cute that we even forgot the execrable smell they produced. After all, these were barnyard animals, with all that implied. As they got older, they lost much of their color and their charm.

Now, here's a puzzle for you. After Easter, we would presumably have to do something with the chicks, which, given the amount of time that passed, and the amount of food provided, were now as big as condors. We couldn't eat them; that would be ghoulish, but here is the puzzle. They were never there to dispose of. Somehow they would disappear at some point before Easter, and we would never have to deal with their disposition.

In later years, we were convinced that Aunt Martha had "gotten rid of them," whatever that meant. While at this late date I am willing to entertain arguments of her innocence, at the time it seemed an adequate explanation. It would be just the type of joke she would love playing.

By this time it would be Holy Week. It would begin with Palm Sunday. In the Maronite Church, this feast rivaled Easter, in splendor if not theological significance. This was the day we would wear our new clothes; we never waited for the Easter Parade or its equivalent. The palms passed out in church provided material for hours of ecclesiastical arts and crafts, as we would use them to create crosses and other religious symbols. We would have a handmade braided-palm cross for every bedroom, to replace the ones we'd made the year before.

The fact that the palm was blessed was a drawback; you couldn't just throw it away. By tradition, it was to be burned. We kids loved the idea because it gave us incipient firebugs a legitimate reason to play with matches. The destruction of outdated palm became a whole other adventure that we managed to complicate more and more each year.

Lent progressed, and on the Tuesday and Wednesday evenings of Holy Week we would have Tenebrae services, the Feast of Lights.

As we prayed and sang, the lights would go out, one by one, and then candles would be relit one at a time to the accompaniment of additional prayers and hymns. Not to waste the darkness — and the lack of supervision by the nuns this late at night — grunts, groans, subdued screams, and scrabbling sounds would permeate the choir pews, as water guns, tacks, and pins came into play in the dark.

On Holy Thursday, an evening Mass would be celebrated — commemorating the Last Supper — and then the altar would be stripped and the images covered in purple cloth in preparation for the Passion and death of Christ.

Next would come Good Friday services, late on Friday afternoon. By this time, we would have completed the ordeal of fasting from twelve noon until three o'clock, by tradition the time Christ spent on the cross.

We, however, went further. (Are you beginning to recognize a pattern here?) The family tradition not only called for abstaining from food and drink during these significant hours, we also were to abstain from speech — we were to keep the Great Silence. We took delight in carrying around pencils and tablets and finding excuses to write messages to each other, often vulgar, thereby, intentionally or unintentionally, defeating the purpose of the spiritual exercise.

One Good Friday we had just enough time to break our fast before we had to be at the religious services of the day. Bob, Dick and I pooled our money; we just managed to afford egg sandwiches from Joe Abraham's, which we commissioned Bob to pick up. He took off to fulfill his vital mission. He returned, opened the door, entered and uttered one of the most famous sentences of our adolescence: "I got something better. I got hot sausage sandwiches."

This, on Good Friday, meatless Good Friday, from the soon-to-be seminarian. After we abused Bob sufficiently, we hid the sandwiches in a refrigerator downstairs that wasn't in use (although Uncle Joe had gotten a great price).

The next morning we had to serve or sing at the Holy Saturday services at dawn. Returning to the house afterwards, famished, we dove for the refrigerator. We had been tasting those sandwiches ever since we had hidden them away the day before.

They were gone.

We halfheartedly berated Bob, but we knew deep down that they had probably gone the way of the peeps. Aunt Martha of the mischievous eyes had struck again.

In all fairness, it is important to note here that, to this day, Aunt Martha stoutly maintains her innocence of both of the foul misdeeds mentioned above.

And then she laughs.

Technically, Saturday marked the end of Lent, but we maintained the seasonal mindset through Holy Saturday with its Midnight Mass, and 11:00 a.m. Solemn High Mass on Easter Sunday. (And don't forget 2:30 Mass.)

Easter Dinner provided little variation, at least in reference to menu, from the other major holidays. The primary difference between Easter and Thanksgiving was that the Easter ham substituted for the Thanksgiving turkey.

The first time I saw Fiddler on the Roof, I couldn't understand the fuss in the opening song explaining and justifying their "traditions." We easily had more, and more inexplicable, family traditions, and nobody ever wrote a song about us, let alone paid to hear one.

*Sr. Rosina awards American Legion Medal to fellow
8th grader Regina Pilardi and me*

Chapter Twelve

Opening Negotiations

The group of salesmen who always gathered at the door of Specialty Clothing, ready to peel off to pick up the next customer, sent for Sam when my grandfather appeared. Sam was my grandfather's salesman; and while, as a salesman, you could prey, you could never poach.

Grampa was there to buy a new suit for Dick, his namesake and oldest grandchild, who followed him in.

This wasn't Downtown at a department store or men's shop. It was Uptown, the wholesale district, often called the "Jewish Strip." Here the tags on clothing contained cryptic lists of numbers that, deciphered properly, identified several different price points. The various price levels reflected frequency of purchase, or amount of money spent, or even the length of acquaintance between the salesman and client. The higher the score on any of these scales, usually, the lower the price.

The final number depended on how effectively you could leverage these, and other factors, during the inevitable negotiating session that preceded many purchases made in the Uptown. My grandfather had worked this area selling wholesale cloth. Several family members shopped regularly at Specialty. Sam had known my grandfather for years. Grampa Rashid, therefore, expected rock-bottom pricing.

Sam approached. "Hello, Rashid!"

"Hello, Sem! I wan' a suit for da boy."

"Da boy" was about ten or eleven at the time and fascinated by the whole process.

They began. Sam showed several suits. Rashid set some aside for further study, and rejected others. Sam brought more. Rashid pulled seams, rubbed fabric, and applied several other obscure tests. He chose a suit, looked at Sam, and queried, "How much?"

"For you Rashid, fifty dollars."

Rashid wasn't impressed.

"I only want one," he replied.

And they engaged.

Through some mystic Middle Eastern process, these skills at negotiation were passed on in the family. It was not only cultural — after all, we were the descendants of Phoenician traders — it was also familial. Almost everyone in the family learned the circumstances under which you bargained for a better price, and how to do so. It stood us in good stead over the years, in financial interactions as diverse as buying a car or a home, or dealing at the flea market or house sale.

Once, on a trip to Europe, I had planned a stop in Brussels, home to the famous Belgian lace industry. Several costume designer friends had requested that I send them some bolts of lace. I sought out the lace district and, accompanied by some friends, headed into one of the shops that had been recommended by the hotel concierge.

The quality of the lace was excellent, so far as I could tell, and the prices seemed good; so my friends began purchasing several bolts. The shop was old-fashioned enough, however, that I had a feeling it would have separate prices for separate clients (especially when I noticed several cryptic numbers attached to each bolt).

I looked for the oldest sales person I could find and my glance landed on an ancient crone looking bored behind the counter. I brought the bolts I had chosen, laid them down before her, and asked if she spoke English. She said yes, so I said I wanted to buy the lace I had chosen, "How much is it?"

She checked the tags and announced a price.

I looked at her and replied with a straight face, "If I pay that much, how will I feed my children?" It didn't really matter that I wasn't even married, let alone a father. It was simply an opening gambit.

Recognizing it for what it was, she immediately became energized, responded with a bright smile, a new price, and added the equivalent of, "One shouldn't have children if one can't afford them."

I suggested a lower price and told her, "It's too late now."

We continued for several minutes, in broken English and broken French, thoroughly enjoying the exchange. We managed to maintain the fiction until we arrived at a price about two-thirds of that paid by my friends. When we parted, both the old woman and I sported a big grin.

Our skills, however, were not infallible. Years after the "suit" incident, my sister/cousin Mariann and her husband Andy were looking to buy a new car. So was I. We both settled on the same model, an AMC Alliance. Mariann and Andy happened to get to the car lot first, worked with the salesman, and bought a new car for what they considered a good price.

The next day, I asked them to accompany me to the same lot, thinking that their experience might give me an edge. I knew what I wanted, so I quickly entered into negotiations. The salesman eventually gave me what he was obviously trained to call the "final" price. It was pretty much the number Mariann and Andy paid the day before. I thought he could beat that. I counter-attacked with a lower number, and threatened to leave, assuming he would come back at me with a lower price.

He looked at me and asked, "After all this time, are you going to walk out of here over a few dollars? What will it take for you to buy this car today?" I knew I had him.

"Are you going to let me walk out of here over a few dollars?" I repeated the figure. He seemed hesitant.

Thinking it would solidify my case, I called Mariann over, expecting some help in administering the final blow. I looked at her and quoted his last offer, the one similar to her cost. I asked something like, "Don't you think they can do better." Her reply, in seeming innocence, floored me. "I don't know. It seems like a pretty good price to me."

I was screwed.

When I asked her later why she hadn't supported me, she replied that she thought it was a pretty good price, and why should I pay less than they did?

I longed for Sam and Specialty Clothing, where the rules were clear.

Girl's Night Out. Left to right:
Cousins: Annie Zagieb,
Martha Kail, Stephanie Niemann
and Helen Kail. Late 1940s at the
Copa in Pittsburgh's Uptown.

Chapter Thirteen

Attention K-Mart Shoppers

The men in our family love to shop. That's like saying that Don Juan liked women, or Genghis Khan enjoyed those occasional military engagements. What's more, the women in the family were smart enough to let the men do the shopping.

I don't mean that Dad occasionally enjoyed stopping at the supermarket or running into the hardware store for a few minutes to pick up some little thing. I mean that my Father loved shopping — for anything. He once bought a whole used drinking fountain — one of those large, enclosed, 4-foot high water coolers with the fountain on top. He fully intended to set it up in the hallway at the house when he got around to it. The kitchen ten feet away with its sink and refrigerator.

"It will be good for the kids," he responded when questioned. "I got a good price."

The water fountain remained in the hall for about four months, unconnected, until my mother or Aunt Martha convinced him that it would be more valuable at the bar.

Or, once he showed up with a large air-conditioning unit. Not a window unit, but a massive machine meant to cool large spaces and whole houses. Unfortunately, it had no compressor, so it couldn't cool anything. It just stood there looking mechanical. I don't know where the air-conditioner-minus-compressor ended up.

"But I got it cheap," he would respond when questioned, and thus declared his adherence to Rule One of "The Kail Family Shopping Code."

1. If it's cheap, buy it.
Whether you need it or not, someone will need it someday.
Or its corollary:
1A. "I got it dirt cheap!" (In that case buy two.)

76

Another of the Kail Family Shopping Rules is:

2. *If you can negotiate a lower price, buy it.* Your commitment of time increases the value. If you spend a lot of time on negotiation, it must be very valuable, or you wouldn't be spending the time.

Rule three is:

3. *Don't run out of anything, ever.*
Thus you need to buy multiples of everything in order to guarantee availability. In our house, we usually had collections of boxes storing toilet tissue or face soap or tomato sauce or paintbrushes. Given a six-month supply of peanut butter, however, we were bound to run out of cheese.

4. *If, each time I buy something for myself, I buy one for someone else as well, it's not an extravagance.*

And rounding out the top five:

5. *"Show no favorites. Everyone gets one."*

And it's not only your responsibility to provide for the family, you must also provide for their friends — and their friends. Thus my Father would buy several of most things, so he could give one to each of the kids, the adults, members of cadet and collateral branches of the family, their neighbors and friends, and people they had once met at a party or bumped into at McDonald's.

My first recollection is clocks; he bought alarm clocks, kitchen clocks, travel clocks, wall clocks. He bought everyone in the family some type of clock. You could never be sure what kind you would receive, but you knew you would be getting one. From clocks, he moved on to transistor radios. They proliferated like mosquitoes. Then came wristwatches. Eventually, my mother would put her foot down, and the inundation would cease — until the next craze began.

Meanwhile, Uncle Joe adhered to the same rules. I remember

one time when he came home with a huge stack of carpenter aprons. They were, of course, valuable to a handyman-about-the-house, but who has ever heard of anyone wearing out a carpenter apron, let alone a dozen of them? When he began giving them away to friends and family, however, their value increased so much that he had to go back and buy more.

"They only cost a quarter!"

Uncle Joe also added shoes. He loved to buy shoes, and not just for himself. I often spent a free afternoon in the Stride-Rite or Buster Brown Shoe Shop with Uncle Joe, looking at my feet through one of those fluoroscope machines that, I'm told, are now illegal. The problem was he also demanded that you take care of the shoes. Like I really wanted to shine my shoes several times a week.

He also discovered towels. Somewhere he found towels for something like ten cents apiece. You can imagine what that triggered.

Dave and Joe loved sales, and they were quite willing to drive ten or twenty miles each way to save five cents on a pound of hamburger or bananas. They lived for the periodic sales on chicken at Verscharen's Market near South Park. When prices reached bottom, they would drive for an hour each way through traffic to stock up on the fowl for both the house and the bar.

Of course, their efforts paled in light of Aunt Genevieve. She would make the round of the shops almost every day — TJ Maxx, Marshall's, Horne's — she had a voracious shopping appetite. Dave and Joe at least had their wives to act as a brake on their shopping propensities. Aunt Gen had Uncle Rege, who was an enabler and a co-dependent.

When Rege passed away, I offered to help Aunt Gen clean out his things to donate to some charity. When I showed up at her home, she pointed me toward the attic. I couldn't even get up the steps to the main room. The entire attic, including the steps, and I mean this literally, was covered to a height of three or four feet with bags and boxes containing clothes and household items they had purchased on one of their shopping forays. And many had never been opened.

It was a bonanza for the St. Vincent de Paul Society and Goodwill. I think Gen and Rege are in their respective Halls of Fame.

Paradoxically, for men who could pinch pennies with the best of them, the Kail brothers were among the most generous of men. They would literally give you the shirt off their backs, and sometimes did.

Uncle Joe did a lot of formal charity, and worked hands-on. He was very active in the St. Vincent de Paul Society, a Catholic charity that did direct work with people and families without resources. He would never admit it, but he tended to be shy. He was uncomfortable stopping at someone's house or apartment carrying the food and clothing, or rent and utility money that would help them to get through the month. Rather than send it with someone else, though, he would enlist Mike or me to accompany him.

Joe also tended to act immediately when he saw someone who needed help. Panhandlers, friends in need, strangers with hard-luck stories — he took all of them at their word. An extremely intelligent man, he would rather look like a fool than risk refusing someone in need. He would reach into his pocket for whatever he had to give. Many times this would be followed by an invitation to the house for a meal.

Dad was the softest touch on Fifth Avenue. Everyone in the Hill District knew that, if you needed real help, Dave or Helen would do their best to provide it, whether it was money, a meal, a job, or a drink, especially if kids were involved.

Mom and Dad sometimes hid their charity from one another. They were really afraid the other would discover just how much money was in play. They would often tell the recipient to be sure not to let the other one know.

Dad obviously lent significant amounts, because, for a long time after his death, repayment sums would dribble in. Mom would shake her head, give a tsk tsk, and comfortably forget that she had at least as much money out there circulating as had my father.

I think they passed on this charitable streak to their children. It seems part of the Kail legacy. We were surprised and amused when, after Dad's death, we discovered that each of us had automatically picked up one of his favorite charities, without telling the others. One took the Little Sisters of the Poor, another took St. Jude's Hospital, and so on.

Formal or informal, the charitable work of the Kail brothers was formidable. But I must admit that, when I'm asked about Dad and Uncle Joe, their intrepid shopping expeditions are what come to mind first.

Chapter Fourteen

Aunt Gen's Eulogy

Then my mother married my father in 1936, she essentially took over running the household. The household at the time consisted of my Grandfather Rashid (barely recovered from the death of his wife), my dad (who had quit Pitt in order to help raise his younger brother and sisters), Philomena (my aunt who was mentally challenged), Genevieve (see below), and Joe. When I say "took over," I literally mean that she assumed responsibility for raising the children, who were all still in school, as well as the responsibility for running the house.

In many ways, she thought of Uncle Joe, Aunt Phil, and Aunt Gen as her own children. I can remember once talking to her about Uncle Joe buying the house next door as office space for the technical sales business he had just opened. Her final comment on the discussion was something like, "Dick and Bob have good jobs, and your business is doing well. If I could just get Uncle Joe settled, I could rest." Uncle Joe was in his fifties at the time.

Philomena was dependent for obvious reasons. She had been severely burned in a fire when she was young. The resulting damage was a great deal of scar tissue and, depending on who told the story, fixation at a mental age of seven or eight. Since many of the details originated with my Aunt Genevieve, we were never quite sure of their accuracy. We were never quite sure if Aunt Phil had been born mentally challenged or if the stories of the fire's effects were accurate. One version of the story had the fire occurring on the Fourth of July, her birthday. Other versions developed that story line further, maintaining that she was sitting on a wagon filled with newspapers, and someone threw some firecrackers onto it.

There was some evidence to support the theory that she had at least started school and, furthermore, went as high as the second grade. The evidence consisted of the fact that she could write her name in script, a skill usually not taught until that grade level in those days.

Aunt Phil, in one sense, seemed to lead an idyllic life. Sheltered from the world, protected from the elements that cause us to lose faith and innocence, in many ways she remained loving and uncorrupted. This, of course, ignores the fact that she never married or had children, never returned to school, and was totally dependent on her father and later my mother and Aunt Martha. I'm not sure she ever realized any of this, because she remained, until her death, almost the embodiment of childhood faith and innocence.

Aunt Genevieve settled in the arms and household of Regis Peter Paul Kennedy. He wasn't Arabic, but he loved her. It took me twenty years to convince my Irish Uncle Regis that, when he visited my home, it was of no use to reach out to shake my hand at the door; he was still going to be hugged.

They were married for thirteen years before they had a child. Maureen was the perfect daughter until she was eighteen, when she became normal.

I believe it was Maureen's twenty-first birthday when I received a call about 2:30 in the morning from Aunt Gen. This is not as odd as it might seem, since she had already established in her mind the fact that I was an expert in all things teen and/or collegiate. Not only had I attended college, but also, on a previous occasion when she had called at 3 a.m., I was able to reassure her that it was in fact true that college libraries were open all night.

In this instance, they were worried because they had left a Happy Birthday message on Maureen's phone, and she hadn't yet called back to acknowledge it. I told them not to expect her before the next day. It was becoming a difficult adjustment for the Kennedys.

As for my Aunt Gen, I provide below an excerpt from the eulogy I delivered for Genevieve Kail Kennedy on December 14, 2002 at St. Philip Church. It is as accurate a picture as I can present of a truly remarkable woman.

My Aunt Genevieve told me that my grandmother, her mother, had died of snakebite. Perhaps it was the dreaded "Squirrel Hill Twister Snake," for I later — much later — found out that my grandmother died in my father's arms, the victim of what was probably an asthma attack.

I would like to talk to you for a few minutes about my Aunt Genevieve — not Mrs. Regis Kennedy, or even Genevieve Kail Kennedy — but my Aunt Gen, everybody's Aunt Gen.

I have spent most of my life dealing with words. I have dined with a Nobel nominated playwright ... and a Poet Laureate of the United States. Neither of them wielded words with the awesome power of my Aunt Gen.

As an English major in college I had to study a linguistic theory that maintained, "Language shapes perception." Well, if language shapes perception, and perception is reality, Aunt Genevieve possessed the God-like quality of shaping reality — of changing the world.

She changed my world. She taught me that "fast food" was cheese and olives, and you could never have too much food around — in case someone dropped in.

She taught me ... to buy the "real thing."

"Yeah, Honey. That's real gold" — or real silver or real wool or real linen.

She taught me that Lebanese was best; Irish was a close second — unless, of course, she was mad at some Lebanese — then the Irish moved into first place. Everybody else bordered on trash. They might even be that most dreaded of epithets — "You Twister, you."

Unless, of course, they were her friends. To them she was ferociously loyal, no matter what the age, race, religion, or country of origin.

Many of her "realities" I later had to unlearn; for instance, the circumstances surrounding the death of her mother, or convincing her daughter that she could speak fluent French. There is one, however, for which I will be eternally grateful. She taught me what was really important.

"They're family, Honey!"

That established her priorities.

And just when I thought I had it all figured out — that I understood just how she manipulated my reality — I realized that she shaped her own reality as well as mine.

I can remember sitting in the hospital with Uncle Rege and Aunt Gen, listening to the doctor explain his medical situation to them. Ten minutes later, Maureen came in and asked what the doctor had said. Aunt Gen's report had nothing to do with what I had heard from the doctor. And, by the time she explained it to Aunt Martha on the phone, it resembled an abstract painting; you knew something was there, but you couldn't quite figure it out.

But, you know what? I didn't care. Because, do you know what I saw happen in that hospital room? I saw my Uncle Rege lean over to my obviously distraught aunt and kiss her cheek and say, "What do you want to do, Hon?"

This from a man that it took me twenty years to teach how to hug.

This eighty-some-year-old man (we never knew his real age) was still very much in love with this seventy-some-year-old woman (Even God never knew her real age.). I wished I could live in that world, in that reality.

Those of you who saw my Aunt Gen's wedding photo — whether at the house or at the funeral home — know that, when she was younger, she was a beautiful woman, even stunning. She never lost that beauty. It just became internalized. She became a bigger woman to contain a much bigger heart.

She was loving, caring, generous, kind, hospitable, sensitive, demanding, exasperating, infuriating — in every sense the queen — of her world.

And, boy, could she shop.

I will always be thankful that she shared her world with me.

I will miss my Aunt Genevieve. I will remember her every time … I eat olives and cheese; when I see Aunt Philomena; when I look at the pictures she stole from my mother's photo album. I will think of her when I hug her daughter Maureen.

I guess she has gone to join Uncle Rege now. She missed him terribly, and I know I should be happy for her. But she has taken with her part of my world, and I mourn its loss.

However, I don't mourn for my Aunt Gen, no matter how much her words shaped my world; because I remember the beginning of John's Gospel: "In the beginning was the Word, and the Word was with God …" And so is my Aunt Genevieve.

Aunt Genevieve and daughter Maureen

Chapter Fifteen

Fitz

J oseph Fitzpatrick was every inch a gentleman, and what minimal claim I have to that same title probably redounds to his credit. He did his best to expose me to the finer things, and to polish (or perhaps grind down) my rough edges.

He was also a gentle man, although he would probably not have acknowledged there was a difference. He had been born in Harrisburg, attended college in Pittsburgh, and remained here to teach art.

Between the ages of twelve and fifteen, I probably spent more time with Fitz than with most of my other friends.

Shortly after we moved to Oakland in the late fifties, Joseph Fitzpatrick, who encouraged us to call him "Fitz," bought the house three doors up from us. I met him on the day he moved in, I saw him carrying armloads of things from the trunk of a car. He was obviously unwilling to entrust them to the moving van that had left earlier. I offered to help unload, he accepted, and the friendship began.

He even looked the part of the gentleman: tall, slender, dignified, ramrod carriage. He had a full head of prematurely white hair, and was always impeccably dressed, albeit often in a style that was slightly out of date. Even when he was painting or gardening he wore khakis and a starched white shirt, and looked well turned out. That phrase, "well turned out," was something he was, and also something he might say.

Fitz was an artist. He was a supervisor in the art program for the Pittsburgh Public Schools, but that was his job. He was an artist. For years, more than a quarter of a century, he also taught in the Saturday morning art classes at Carnegie Museum, where his students included the young Andrew Warhola, eventually to resurface in New York as Andy Warhol.

Friendship with Fitz often comprised a series of mundane tasks, none of which I had ever performed before, as well as some esoteric activities I was never to perform again.

While he did some excellent sculptures, his primary medium was oil or acrylics. His paintings were dark, angular, colorful, often allegorical, stylized or abstract, but not obscure. They were immediately pleasing to the eye.

His house was divided into two apartments; his was on the ground floor. His portion of the house was painted stark white, although he called it "eggshell white," and that became my first lesson in observation. He acknowledged that my medium was probably language and his was paint, but he stressed the need to "see." "To observe is the beginning of creating art."

When his tenants moved, he never rented the upstairs apartment again. He used part of it as a studio. He decorated his home mostly with his own artwork, plus a gorgeous carved wooden carousel pony that sat in his living room as a permanent element of the décor.

He liked for me to sing, although he was careful not to fan the flames of vanity, and I would often sing when performing manual labor. And we did a lot of manual labor. Our houses sat at the foot of a large hill, one of the many things for which Pittsburgh is noted. Attached to the rear of each home was about a hundred feet of "undeveloped" hill; Fitz was about to bring his hundred feet into cultivation, and I, more or less willingly, was to assist.

We spent a great deal of time in the dirt.

It took us months to get the first plants in. The hill was strewn with rocks and boulders that had to be dug up and moved to fit his vision. We then established pockets of fertile soil that would serve as home and shelter to a variety of plants that was beyond anything I had ever seen.

Some of the plants were left in pots to control their growth. When Fitz explained this, I realized that he actually had, not just a vision, but also a completed design in mind. I had thought we were just digging a lot and using whatever spaces were available to plant.

Mike would occasionally help when he was home, and I think several of the other kids might have pitched in a few times as well.

The work of the additional laborers, however, was offset by Mrs. Trotier, his next-door neighbor. She gave him the gift of her hill. "I never use that part of the property," she said. "I'd love to have it look as good as yours."

Later, after we completed the original design, several local newspapers and magazines covered the garden in a series of articles. All of them featured somewhere in the headline or body the theme of "The Hanging Gardens," although this was definitely not Babylon and there was nothing hanging.

Fitz's vision included constant updating and improvement. Long after I left home, he was still working on it.

I have worked on several large projects in my life, but Fitz's garden was the most intense and difficult over the longest period of time. I don't know if he knew me that well and that quickly, but that type of project was exactly what I needed at that age. It helped teach me discipline and perseverance. And the interaction with him provided insights it would have been difficult to learn elsewhere.

Fitz became an anomaly in the neighborhood. He lived directly across the street from St. Agnes Church, but was an active member at St. Paul Cathedral Parish. He was elegant and soft-spoken, and never failed to greet all of his neighbors, so he was popular. Yet Fitz seldom visited any house in the neighborhood, although he was frequently invited. At most, he might stop over and stand on our steps for a few minutes visiting with my mother or Uncle Joe. I don't think he ever entered our home.

My mother was a special favorite of his. He frequently expressed to me the desire to paint her, but knew she would be too self-conscious, and could never sit still for that long. Actually, every artist I knew, and that eventually became a large number, expressed the desire to paint my mother. It took me years before I began to see in my own mother the beauty they noticed almost immediately.

I, on the other hand, spent hours in his company and in his home. We would spend most of the time in his kitchen seated in a large breakfast nook upholstered in red vinyl. Looking back, he was either very lonely or very kind, probably both. He never said an angry word to me (and I have been told I can sometimes be infuriating). He was unfailingly courteous and demanded the same of me. He would never accept anything crass or in bad taste, perhaps sensing that I had not yet developed a sense of what was crass or in bad taste. His disapproval was indicated by a drawn-out "Oooh, Eugene!"

We talked about a lot of things. Politically, he was pretty conservative; but in his personal relationships he was very accepting. He was surprised at how well read I was, and I explained a bit about Central Catholic High School, which I attended, as well as its forensics program. This led him to ask a lot of questions about the school, and I later realized that he was asking as an educator, not just as a friend. He often spoke highly of the art program at Central, though I never knew how he knew.

He had a wide variety of friends, many of whom I met at one time or another. I'm not sure how, or even if, he explained me to them, but they were accepting of me as well. While they ranged from working class to wealthy, they were unfailingly polite and genteel.

Fitz did not drive. He was the only Pittsburgher I ever knew who travelled consistently by cab. He even went food shopping in a cab. Once I learned to drive, I often did errands for him, and learned a lot about trust. He would often hand me a wad of bills to pay for something or other, and never count the change. He would simply throw it in the drawer where he obviously kept a great deal of cash.

One of the last major tasks I performed for him was the most interesting. He was invited to mount a show of his artwork at the Pittsburgh Center for the Arts. He didn't really have the time, and asked if I would help put it together. I glibly said "yes," not realizing what would be involved.

He first chose works from among those pieces he had at his house. He then added a few pieces that he had sold over the years. Every decision taught me more about art and business. But I was to learn a great deal more.

Fitz handed me a list of names and addresses and a wad of bills. He then charged me with traveling by taxi to the homes of the owners of the works he had indicated on the list. I was to pick up the artworks and deliver them to the site of the show. Some of the homes I visited are now museums themselves. Families representing several of the major fortunes of Pittsburgh collected his paintings and sculptures.

Finally, I helped him hang the show and acted as guide over the several weeks it lasted. I like to say that I sold several of his paintings, but, in truth, they were sold because of their quality and potential value. He did, however, give me a commission on the paintings sold.

What an experience! I was fifteen.

By this time, although I was not a polished member of the gentry, I at least knew they existed, and I had met several of them, and had actually spoken to a few. We gathered years later at St. Paul Cathedral for his funeral, bound by affection for an artist and a gentleman.

That's how I learned what it meant to be a gentleman. It had little to do with money or birth status. It had a lot to do with a tall, white-haired man from West Oakland who was kind to a young neighbor thirsty for what he had to offer.

Chapter Sixteen

Meet the Parents

If you have been reading these tales in order, you obviously have had to gain some insight into my mom and dad, as well as Aunt Martha and Uncle Joe, my surrogate parents. They are, at the same time, both every day present and seemingly larger than life, and also private, complex, and elusive. I guess any son might make similar observations about his parents.

My mother and father were an odd blend of orthodoxy and conventional behavior on the one hand and independent thinking on the other. They had also pretty much reversed the traditional male and female roles: Mom was a realist, Dad a romantic. Mom frequently hid her emotions, Dad tended to wear his on his sleeve. Mom made the tough decisions, or at least that's how it seemed on the surface. We later realized that my mother never made a really important decision without deferring to my father

Both of them were devoutly Catholic, praying every day, attending Mass every Sunday and often on other days, especially if one of the kids were serving Mass that week. They bought the theology and the philosophy as thoroughly as did the clergy, and their religious orthodoxy was beyond question.

For their fortieth wedding anniversary, we thought it would be nice to have a family Mass in an intimate setting. In those immediately post-Vatican II days the strictures about time and place for Mass seemed to be relaxed, or at least not enforced. We prevailed upon Father Ward, a friend of the family since his seminary days with my brother Bob, and he agreed to say Mass at Bob's apartment.

At Communion time, both Mom and Dad refused the host, very unusual for them. Well, of course, we weren't going to let that drop. We kept questioning them until they admitted that they had risen early and gone to 6 a.m. Mass, where they had received Communion. They weren't too sure about this Mass-in-the-apartment stuff.

On the other hand, they ran a bar in one of the worst areas of the city, with all the compromised morality that suggests about their patrons. They both gambled regularly. And, for some reason, they were also very liberal in the way they raised us. They seldom gave us a curfew, and as long as they knew where we were — or thought they did — it was OK if we got home late, sometimes very late.

They never used corporal punishment as a disciplinary device, and they seldom raised their voices at us. I can remember only once being slapped by either of them. Rather, they showed disapproval in a couple of ways. They might calmly ask a simple question or make a simple statement that showed their disapproval. "Are you really going to do that?" or, more profoundly, "It's not right."

More frequently, and just as devastatingly, they gave us "the look." There were several "looks" that varied by situation. There was the "I can't believe I raised such a stupid son" look. Or the look that indicated, "It's your responsibility to do something" (e.g., invite someone to dinner, offer to drive them somewhere, offer to perform some errand, etc.). But the disciplinary look showed so much hurt in the eyes, so much pain, disappointment, and regret, that it made it almost impossible to travel further along the road to perdition that you had obviously begun.

I have a sneaking suspicion that my parents realized early on that they had three sons who were independent and intelligent, but not very malleable, at least by traditional methods. I'm not sure how, but they transferred to us an acute sense of right and wrong. We seldom discussed it. And I'm not even sure they trained us by example. I think it had something to do with positive behaviors and positive reinforcement. They were not angels or saints, but most of the time they simply did what was right.

Neither of them was raised this way, so I have always been curious about how they decided on this approach. Furthermore, they both used these methods, and that made it even more curious.

My mother had obviously been raised with a consciousness of the middle-class virtues. She knew the protocols for traditional functions such as teas and receptions; and, when she was able, she would attend them, especially when they were attached to school or family.

Despite the fact that she worked a six-day week for fifty years, Mom liked to maintain the fiction that she would rather be a simple housewife — as if there were such a thing. We all thought she would become bored to death within a month. One Sunday she was cooking breakfast for my dad. I, jokingly, maintained to my mother he should be cooking breakfast for her, since she worked just as hard as he did. It was one of the few times my mother jumped all over me. I had never seen such a lightning change in her demeanor. She adamantly informed me that it was her "duty" to cook for her husband. I think she somehow felt that working at the bar didn't count. Her primary identity — even her primary reality — was as my father's wife and mother of a family.

Mom did her best to support us in everything we did, whether she understood it or not. By the time we were in high school, she went out infrequently, and didn't really like the theatre, but she seldom missed one of my plays, especially if it were a musical. Neither she nor my dad had the slightest idea what "forensics" was all about, but she would be sure to ask how I had done each time I returned from a tournament. They both made any number sacrifices so that I could make expenses for the trips we took on the busy debate circuit. She even attended the Forensic Banquet at the end of each year. The only time she thought of not attending was when she found out that that year's banquet was in her honor.

My dad, on the other hand, because of his deafness and his working hours, seldom attended anything we did. I think he went to one sports banquet for Dick and my commencement at Duquesne. Ironically, the only reason I attended was because he was coming.

Dad didn't like "going out" in the traditional sense. It was too much trouble. The last time I can remember him spending a traditional evening out was to see the movie The Godfather in the seventies, more than a decade before he passed away.

He did, however, enjoy going out to dinner. His preference, of course, would be a "steak and potatoes" menu at a "good" restaurant. When we noticed our parents getting older, Bob, Dick, and I made a concerted effort to get them out to dinner every couple of months.

We were happy that we did. Of course, Dad would head for his bar after we left the restaurant. He would say that he had to set up for the next day. We knew that he was meeting his cronies.

In a family addicted to sarcasm, practical jokes, and laughter, Mom had little sense of humor, and seldom laughed. Dad, on the other hand, was a real tease. Despite his reluctance to spend time away from home and work, he was a favorite among the extended family. My Uncle Dave in Dayton would regale us with tales of my father making the eight-hour drive from Pittsburgh to court my mother, and arriving wearing a T-shirt, slacks, and house slippers.

I think they respected his integrity and perseverance, but especially an odd type of dignity. He seldom spoke, seldom had much money, but he was fiercely loving and loyal to family and friends. Even the children liked him. I think they all sensed his affection.

His sense of humor sometimes compromised the impact of "the look." My cousin Judy, while visiting from Rochester, stayed out one night until a ridiculously late hour. At sixteen, she considered herself an adult. Dad didn't think she could even spell "adult." She was a victim of the double standard that permeated most of the Mediterranean cultures. As males, we could come and go at will. It was different for girls.

Judy found herself in a dilemma. She had no key, and it was after 2 a.m., so she didn't want to ring the bell and wake the house. Her solution: climb in the front window, jump on the couch, and sneak up the stairs to bed. My father, however, after closing the bar and coming home, had fallen asleep on the couch. A high heel in the stomach woke him instantly. When he finally figured out the situation, his discipline was undermined by the fact that Judy let out a guffaw that could wake Lazarus. He tried "the look," but couldn't keep from laughing.

I think my father had an unerring sense of right and wrong; he seldom saw the gray. Although he sometimes felt compelled to act pragmatically, I could never tell if this caused him pain or if he simply accepted its occasional necessity.

Like Dad, my mother was the oldest sibling in her family, and was also well respected. Despite the fact that she lived 250 miles away from her mother and siblings, few decisions about her mother would be made without her input.

As a child, I was upset because my mother seemed to shout a lot, although not at me. It took me a long time to realize that she was not shouting in anger or frustration, but was merely raising her voice because my dad was becoming progressively more deaf.

Dad's deafness was a fact of life. He had bought hearing aids early on, but found them uncomfortable, so he gave them to us to play Captain Video and Space Cadet. Until years later, when he found hearing aids that fit into the ear and worked fairly well, we simply had to shout. I didn't realize it until years later, but my friends were puzzled by me shouting at my father.

My dad was also popular with my friends, because he would often be sarcastic with them, treating them as peers. He called them all "kiddo," because he seldom remembered names. Many of them said they had interesting conversations with him, but it was questionable; he simply couldn't hear them. What he had perfected, however, was a sort of inchoate mumble that passed for conversation.

Both very generous people, my parents sometimes hid their charity from each other, not wanting to let it be known how much money was in play. They both were the proverbial "soft touch." The same was true of their gambling. They hid the amounts from each other. They both played the numbers, and my dad also frequently bet on sports. For years my mother's number was 101, the address of their former grocery store.

I didn't really realize it until I began thinking about writing this description, but one of the things I remember most about the two of them together was that they were together. They were DaveandHelen. Even into their seventies, there was an affection between them. They touched each other all the time. They argued frequently, but I think it had simply become their method of communication. And my dad would never leave the house without kissing my mother, even in the middle of a disagreement.

Neither of them seemed given to introspection, but then who really knows his parents. Either of them could have had a whole secret life. But if you asked either of them to summarize their lives and give a judgment, both of them would have told you to go to hell.

• • •

Aunt Martha and Uncle Joe, on the other hand, would have different reactions. Mart would laugh and tell you it was none of your business. Joe would sit down with you for a long discussion, ending with an invitation to dinner, followed by another invitation to join the family in reciting the Rosary along with this week's designated priest on the radio.

Obviously, with Mom and Dad working a six- or seven-day week, and a ten- to twelve-hour day, we were often left in the care of Aunt Martha and Uncle Joe, unique in their own way.

How do I describe Aunt Martha? She is short. She is sharp. She is pretty. She is old. She had seven children.

How do I explain Aunt Martha? She tends not to gossip, keeps things to herself. She has a temper under control. She doesn't bear fools well. She plays her cards close to the vest. She is a good listener, but she seldom shows how she feels. She loves playing jokes on people.

And she's a devil.

It's all right there in her eyes.

I have a copy of Aunt Mart 's First Communion photo. It's a studio photo, taken sometime in the late 1920s. What is remarkable about it is not the beautiful period dress, or the sweet smile. It's her eyes. Everyone who sees the photo, even without knowing Martha, comments on the look in her eyes. Some call it mischievous. Others call her a devil.

I'm perfectly willing to admit that I would probably use that term simply for effect; however, it is highly descriptive of her personality,

She is ninety-three years old now, and her once-perfect complexion shows a few wrinkles. Her hair has some gray in it, but it is still primarily dark; so, like my grandmother, she is accused of coloring it.

It is hard to remember that, when we were kids, and she was

newly married, she used to put on a pair of jeans and wrestle with us kids on the floor. It's hard to remember that she once threatened to put her fist through the cake at a birthday party if the kids didn't quiet down; and she did. It's hard to remember that she once threatened to empty a bowl of cereal, including milk, on Dick's head, when he wouldn't believe she was serious; and she did. And we loved her for it, and we laughed, never believing for a moment that there was anything malicious involved. (Actually, it really isn't hard to remember; we tell the stories all the time, but I like the rhetorical device.).

Because she is so quiet and unassuming, some people seem to think that she was simply a dutiful wife, living vicariously through Uncle Joe. Yet those who really know her remain completely convinced of her intelligence, her toughness, and her sense of humor. Like my mother, she seems satisfied with the conscious decision to let her husband shine, and to accept the role of the dutiful wife. However, where Mom would bluster until it became time to defer to my father, Aunt Mart simply kept her own counsel. If she contradicted Uncle Joe, she must have done it in private.

Like my parents, they were brought up with traditional values and fairly conventional behaviors. However, at least with Uncle Joe, those values and behaviors stuck. Unlike my parents, for instance, Joe and Martha did believe in corporal punishment.

With Aunt Martha, it wasn't a problem. Although she would grab the handiest weapon with which to administer corporal punishment — a wooden spoon, a ping-pong paddle — the actual delivery of the punishment could be forestalled by placing your outstretched hand on her head. Since she was only about four-feet-ten-inches tall, no matter how much she swung, you remained out of reach and essentially untouchable. And if you could get her to laugh, which wasn't that hard, you were home free.

Uncle Joe found us eminently touchable and would administer punishment for various transgressions. This wasn't a problem, unless he had lost his temper. Then the physical punishment became very physical. I was about fourteen, in the midst of being hit for some reason or other; Joe was chasing me up the stairs with additional corporal punishment in mind. I suddenly had enough. I stopped, turned to him and said, "Don't ever hit me again." And he never did.

He was such a kind and generous man that I was puzzled by his temper, and the speed with which he would fly off the handle, especially when driving. We often seemed to be tiptoeing around him. This seemed out of character. As I grew older, I sometimes wondered if we were seeing some residual effects of his participation in World War II. Joe fought actively in the Pacific, landing in the first wave on both Leyte and Okinawa. He received both the Bronze Star and The Purple Heart. Until very late in life, he would seldom talk about the war, except perhaps to snort at the inaccuracy of most Hollywood portrayals of combat.

Other than this flaw of temper, I sincerely believe that Uncle Joe consciously strove to be what I can only call a Christian gentleman. Like the other three parents, he was devoutly religious. He seldom, if ever, questioned his faith; but, as a long-term member of the Newman Club at Carnegie Mellon University, he searched to find its intellectual underpinnings, often attending lectures and performing acts of charity.

Like his brother, my dad, Joe was very generous, frequently buying us shoes or clothes and always responding positively when asked for help. And also like his brother he had a pronounced sense of hospitality; he invited quite literally everybody to stay/come to dinner. He enjoyed guests and enjoyed showing off his family.

The relationships among the four parents were fascinating to outsiders. They thought it a unique situation, and it was. The patience and affection that had to underlay their interrelationships must have worn thin at times, but they made it work. What fascinated those on the outside looking in was somewhat different from what fascinated me on the inside. I wanted to know who these people were.

It was helpful that I was the only one of the four oldest children who remained at home into adulthood. Dick married at eighteen. Bob and Mike spent much of their adolescence in the seminary and didn't spend much time at home, even during breaks. My insights and understanding about the "four parents" were the result of long observation and adult interaction.

I found that I could talk to my dad when he would drive me to various destinations — especially the airport, which he often did. It began a habit of interaction that I treasure. During one drive, he asked how I preferred to travel. I said that I preferred the train. He replied that was "so nineteenth century." He preferred to fly. With the image of T-shirt and slippers in mind, I laughed, and teased that he had never even been on an airplane.

He replied with "the look" and told the story of joining with two friends to buy a used airplane (in what had to be the late twenties or early thirties), and flying coast to coast, putting down every few hundred miles to work for food and gas money. This from the guy who panicked when I was a few minutes late returning from an out-of-town trip. I was flabbergasted, and not for the only time.

I really came to understand Uncle Joe more as an adult, because I was the only one who would accompany him on various "excursions" around the city. He seemed actually to be very shy, and would often "push too hard" in order to compensate. He was relieved when I would go with him to fulfill his charitable duties, delivering aid through the St. Vincent de Paul Society and other groups. I would also go with him to lectures at the Newman Club, where an esoteric topic united rather than puzzled us. And he loved it when I would accompany him on a shopping expedition, especially with nothing particular in mind

Aunt Martha was more difficult to get to know as a person. She seldom expressed what she really felt, and was curiously guarded in her thoughts and judgments. For instance, while Uncle Joe was nominally a lifelong Democrat, as he aged he leaned more and more toward Republican conservatism in his conversation and voting. Aunt Martha, on the other hand, would seldom discuss her vote, yet on more than one occasion suggested — more by omission or a fleeting glance — that she had voted liberal Democrat.

I tried to spend some time with Mart as she grew older, just talking about family and her experiences as a child. She eventually felt comfortable enough to begin to go deeper. I think, once she saw she could trust me not to pass it on as gossip, she became much less guarded in her conversation, and eventually even came around to an occasional criticism of her own kids, something she would never do when she was younger.

One of my great regrets is that I really didn't come to know my mother very well as a person until the brief decline before her death, when we would take turns being with her in her bedroom around the clock. This heart-rending scenario became a sort of perverse gift, as we would occasionally talk when she couldn't sleep.

She would seldom question me directly, couching her concerns in discussions of more innocuous topics. Thus, when watching her favorite TV program, "Touched by an Angel," she might ask whether I believed in angels or an afterlife. It fascinated me that this woman, who had been forced to deal with so much of the seamy side of life, had preserved so much innocence and religious faith. She often prayed the Rosary along with a tape I had bought her.

She loved the sister/cousins dearly. I think some of her happiest moments at this point were when their children came to spend time with her. They were delightful with her, and I think she felt they somehow justified all of the difficulties over the years.

One night she made me promise to make sure that Aunt Martha could stay in the house as long as she wanted, and reminded me to keep the family together, no matter what arguments might arise. She sometimes said these things as though I weren't there, almost as if they were a litany of "things to take care of." I could just as easily have been Bob or Dick or Mike or Mariann. She just couldn't lay down her burden.

This is by far the longest story in this collection. All I can say is that all of my parents deserve it. It is my thank-you gift for what they gave me, what they made me — not the gift of telling a story that is actually more mine than theirs — but for the gift of the family, and for making me care enough to want to know them and share them as individuals, and trying to get it right.

Martha and Joe wedding day. Dorothy Thomas (Martha's sister) and Dave Kail witness the nuptials.

My parents' wedding

Chapter Seventeen

Rheumatic Fever

Throughout this book, if you pay attention, you will see the phrase "rheumatic fever" (note that I do not give it the respect of a capital letter). I'm not sure that I can accurately describe it or its implications, but, since it had such an impact on my life, I thought it important to try.

Sister Mary Robert suggested to my mother that I was ready for kindergarten at the age of four, so Mom sent me. This turned out to be a lucky break, because I was to miss the next year and more to an attack of rheumatic fever. Essentially, the disease is an inflammation of the heart that causes valve damage, an enlarged heart, and a weakened state. I was in the hospital for two weeks.

The bad news was that I couldn't walk. I was profoundly fatigued, and I became bedridden for more than a year. The good news was that I was alive, and that we had entered the age of antibiotics. Penicillin and Streptomycin saved my life, I was told. (Please note the capital letters.) I took a daily dose of penicillin until I was in my thirties. It was part of a longitudinal study sponsored by the County Health Department. We were the first generation to have these drugs available, and they were still investigating dosages, duration, etc.

Given the size of the family, there was not an extra room to use as a "sickroom." I stayed in the "boys' room" and shared a bed. Since, even then, our house was the one where everyone hung out, I really didn't miss much. Every day, for some amount of time, my brothers and the neighborhood kids could be found playing in the room.

Dr. Louis Kochin, a wonderful pediatrician, was my family doctor until he passed away when I was in my twenties. He closely monitored my progress. Dr. Kochin was a throwback to an earlier time, even in the fifties when all of this was occurring. He was both a rabbi and a pediatrician. And he still made house calls. The charge was $5 for an office visit and $10 for a house visit, period. No matter what he did — shots, eye and ear exam, vaccinations — the charge remained the same. He didn't keep written records, which caused a bit of a problem after he died, but, while he was alive, he had a voluminous memory, and could recall every patient and the treatment he had provided.

Realizing that I wasn't receiving the amount of rest I needed, Kochin looked for a way to keep me in bed and resting more. At one point he had a major brainstorm, a television. TV was still in its infancy; no one in the neighborhood had one. I read later that, in those years, there were fewer than 750,000 TVs in the country. Kochin felt that, if I had a TV, I would lie still and watch it.

Since there was a delivery strike going on at the time, my dad had to buy the TV at Kaufmann's Department Store, carry it to his car, drive home, and wrestle it up two flights of stairs to the boys' room. The TV was a leather-covered, table model Zenith with a twelve-inch circular screen. I remember the first TV program I ever saw; it was an episode of "The Cisco Kid" starring Duncan Renaldo and Leo Carrillo.

Soon we discovered the flaw in Dr. Kochin's reasoning. As the first TV in the neighborhood, it acted as a magnet for the neighbors. Rather than cause me to rest more, it caused a great deal more excitement. Now we not only had children showing up to play, we also had adults having their first interaction with the TV screen.

And at 7:30 p.m., when I was supposed to retire for the night, the crowd watching the TV, rather than leave the room, would simply tell me to roll over and go to sleep. I, of course, developed the technique of watching TV from under my elbow. I was determined not to miss a thing.

As I gradually recovered, Dr. Kochin searched for a way for me to get the amount of rest he felt I needed. Eventually I was able to spend more and more time out of bed; because of my atrophied muscles, I had to undergo an early form of physical therapy in order to walk again. I was still in bad shape.

It looked as if my family was going to have to send me to a facility called the "Heart House," where I could get the care I needed in an atmosphere where there was minimal excitement. I would be forced to live in a "facility," with strangers, and spend most of the day resting. You can imagine my excitement.

And then Doctor Kochin had another brainstorm. Why not send me to stay with my grandparents in Ohio? There were no kids there, and it would be a restful setting in which I could recover.

I spent the next year or more with my grandparents in Dayton. Every year after that, until I was fifteen, I would leave for Dayton in June, after school let out, and return home in September, in time to go back to school.

As a result of this childhood illness, I was prevented from playing sports; I was excused from gym class; I spent a lot of time reading; I was treated differently from other kids and, in general, underwent the kinds of experiences that would guarantee that I wasn't going to be an MMA fighter or an offensive lineman.

Obviously, I missed a lot while I was in Ohio, but I also gained a great deal as well. Since most of my time was spent with my grandparents and their friends, I became very comfortable in the company of adults. This stood me in good stead later, when I discovered girls and began meeting the parents of my dates.

I also learned to cook and to speak Arabic, not necessarily at the same time. I became close to my aunts, uncles and cousins in Dayton. I even learned to dance the traditional Arabic dances. The influence was profound and pervasive.

Pope John XXlll was fond of saying, "When God closes a door, He opens a window." In my case, He did. It's not the window I would have chosen — and the length of time it took to open left something to be desired — but it did open.

They also say that God never gives you a burden that you are not capable of carrying. In my case, He skated pretty close to the edge.

Chapter Eighteen

A Popular History of Lebanon

*T*he following is called "A Popular History of Lebanon" because it was popular in my family. This has no bearing on its veracity or accuracy; popularity has little to do with truth. I cite it here, because it is what we were raised believing. It has taken me some struggle to get it down on paper, because I don't ever remember hearing it articulated in any kind of order, with any kind of thoroughness. It is essentially just bits and pieces I gleaned over the years from various sources, with varying degrees of accuracy and various levels of bias.

There are obvious inaccuracies. For example, the explanations of the origins of the country known as Lebanon are obscure, at best, despite the fact that we saw a direct line to the Phoenicians. The involvement with the French obviously has to predate World War I. And the interactions among the Turks, the Syrians, and the Lebanese were much more complex than rendered here, let alone the interactions among the Maronites and the Muslims, whether Shi'ite or Sunni, or the Druze.

Nevertheless, this was "our" history in a very real sense. It was what we considered our heritage, at least early on. Possibly I should call it "My Popular History of Lebanon."

A Popular History of Lebanon

Lebanon is an ancient country composed of several different, but related, cultures. Many of its primary contributions come from the Phoenicians, with their culture of trade and exploration, and also other influences, such as the Hittites and Philistines of Biblical note. It was Hiram, King of the Phoenicians, who brought to Solomon the great Cedars of Lebanon to build the Temple. Many of the Mediterranean coastal settlements that later became major cities were founded by these far-ranging voyagers. Cadiz and Carthage were among them, making Hannibal an early Lebanese warlord.

At the time of the late nineteenth- and early twentienth-century immigration, different political realities prevailed. First, as Lebanon developed as a national entity, she, of course, became Arabic-speaking, but there were strong western strains in her culture.

For example, while most of the Arabic world necessarily developed into a desert culture, Lebanon was a fertile country of mountains and green valleys. Looking westward, she made the basis of her economy to be trade and finance. Lebanon eventually became a large banking and financial center, and its capital of Beirut was often called the "Paris of the Middle East" for its beauty. Of course, many Lebanese considered Paris the Beirut of the West.

Furthermore, while in most of the Arabic world, Islam took hold and flourished, in Lebanon the Maronite branch of the Catholic Church developed from a solid base laid in the first and second centuries. It eventually became so prevalent that, at the time of Lebanese independence from the French in the late 1940s, Lebanon's new constitution stated that the president must come from among the Maronite community.

For many years, Lebanon was ruled by Syria under the Ottoman Turks. For this reason, many of the Lebanese who migrated in the late nineteenth and early twentieth centuries did so on a Syrian passport, and identified themselves as Syrian. Australia, Brazil, and the United States were the three major destinations for this Lebanese diaspora.

The mountains and valleys of Lebanon constitute a series of natural enclaves, often ruled by "warlords" with private armies. Eventually, these local leaders associated themselves with either the Moslem or Christian factions.

Since Lebanon's independence from the French — who had been ceded control of the country by the League of Nations after World War I — the country's territory has been a chaotic crossroads for the violent political confrontations playing out in the Middle East. Thus Syria, Israel, the Palestinians, the Jordanians, ISIS, and other forces have controlled, and still control, various parts of Lebanese geography, constituting a strong, continuing, and discomfiting foreign presence on Lebanese soil. Even the United States' attempts to maintain a sphere of influence. These forces do not remain neutral, but exert almost unbearable pressure on the Lebanese people to support one or another of the factions.

The violence and bloodshed of the last half-century have ravaged the tiny country. In the past several years, bombings, rocket and mortar attacks and political assassinations have become daily facts of life. And there is no one to come to the rescue.

Grandma Betrosea, "She was loved."

Chapter Nineteen

Grandma and the Parallel Back-Formation

My grandmother Bitrosea (pronounced Bitrosea) had a way with language that wreaked havoc with linguistic niceties.

First of all, there was the alphabet. The two alphabets — Arabic and English — are hugely different, and the characters of each often symbolize sounds that don't exist in the other language, so pronunciation becomes a major issue.

When having a conversation with my grandmother, you had to be alert not only to what she said, but also to what she meant, making her sort of the Yogi Berra of Lebanese-Americans. This was not always easy. One of her most obvious linguistic idiosyncrasies was in creating "back-formations," taking an American word and treating it as if it were Arabic.

One day I went to visit her. She was engrossed in the TV, watching what she called "my stories." I waited quietly for her to acknowledge me. At the first commercial of the program, she felt bound to provide a summary. She had been watching a war movie, she explained in Arabic, in which the paratropia fought behind the German lines. In pronouncing the word paratropia, she had substituted the b sound for the p sound, added a rolled r, a dentalized t, and the stress on the penultimate syllable, i. It finally became clearer to me after I reversed the linguistic process. I replaced the p sound, unrolled the r, eliminated the dentalizing on the t, and turned the ia ending back into its English cognate s, and got a story about paratroopers.

At the time she left Lebanon, paratroopers did not exist, either in word or in person. Her linguistic solution to the unfamiliar word was to add an Arabic plural ending and the Arabic pronunciation, to make the word hers.

We grandchildren became fond of collecting her linguistic gems and sharing them. For example, if we were carrying on during dinner, she would stand up to her full four-foot-ten, smack her open palm on the table, and admonish us, "Don' make fun on Jesus' table." That put a whole new light on our bickering.

If we were arguing over nothing — simply making noise to hear our own voices (a fairly frequent occurrence) — her response was, "Wucha diffrin, Honey, bot' same t'ing." (What's the difference, Honey? They are both the same thing.)

In Middle Eastern culture, the virtue of hospitality is held in high esteem. If it moves, you feed it, or hug it, or both. A refusal to stuff yourself at her dinner table would elicit from Grandma, "Eat, Honey, eat. Don' be strange." Dropping the article a and the final r in "stranger" held no significance for my grandmother in delivering her message.

One of her grandchildren — me — was held out of school for a year with a major illness. I had started school early and later skipped a grade, so it all worked out. My grandmother, however, often confused age with grade level. When introducing me to a friend, she was likely to explain, "He's ten. He woulda been 'leven, but he was sick for a year."

When we misbehaved, which was about as often as normal kids, my grandmother would threaten us with a fate whose origins were lost in obscurity. Essentially, she would threaten to give us to the dogcatcher. However, the dogcatcher worked for an organization called the Animal Rescue League. In Grandma's lexicon the phrase came out something like "Emeresky," with a rolled r, of course. How seriously could you take a disciplinary system based on a four-foot-ten elderly woman chasing you through the house shouting, "I'm gonna call da Emeresky."

To avoid charges of sexism, or possibly a smack in the head with a rolled newspaper from one of the six female siblings, I suppose I ought to tell a grandfather language story.

My oldest brother Dick had his first real girlfriend. She was tall and lanky, not what you would call the Middle Eastern ideal. (That ran somewhere along the lines of a Queen Latifah or a Shelley Winters in later life.) Dick maintained she looked like a high-fashion model. Most of his friends simply called her skinny.

He brought her home one day to meet my Grandfather Rashid,

who took one look, turned to me and said, in Arabic, "Mu'ffee shee" (loosely translated as, "There's nothing there.") That not only settled the argument, it provided a nickname. From then on, people took to calling her Muffy.

By paying attention over the years to my grandparents' speech, I learned some things about language that they don't teach you in class (pretty valuable, since much of my professional life has been language-based).

- When you swear in a foreign language, it sounds less harsh. The most lurid curses sound sort of cute.
- What is horrifying in a foreign language may be innocuous in English and vice versa. One of the worst things my grandmother could say about another was that the person came from bite bu claib, ("house of the dogs"). When I was younger, that also sounded sort of cute.
- Being able to speak some foreign language, no matter how rudimentary your skill, impresses women. Of course, it helps if the language is exotic and the woman is drunk. German and Latin get you nowhere, but Arabic is hot. (Not that I would take unfair advantage of this tendency, only fair advantage, especially if she's cute.)
- Some men of Middle Eastern heritage have not yet grown beyond adolescent sexism.

I spent a great deal of time with my grandmother and have a great number of memories. Some of the richest are sensory rather than intellectual, the sound of her laugh, deep in her throat; the smell of the single daily cigarette she smoked at breakfast, using her daily grapefruit peel as her ashtray; her very dark hair, worn the same for most of her life, and which people accused her of coloring well into her eighties. (She didn't.)

One of my most delightful memories is that of my grandmother playing hostess to Shirley when Dick brought her to Dayton to meet the family. In honor of Shirley, of whom she was immensely proud — she called her "Shilly" — Grandma finally "came out" of mourning for my grandfather, who had died almost a decade before.

We were attending the wedding of the daughter of one of her friends. She was there to show off Shirley; so, for the first time in years, she didn't wear black.

When we entered the reception, the whole roomful of people, in a spontaneous outburst of affection, rose to their feet and applauded. Dick and Shirley and I were confused, not understanding the significance of the ovation. Grandma just blushed slightly, turned to us, and said simply, "Don' worry, Honey, dat's for me."

My grandmother was one of the strongest people I ever knew, both physically and emotionally. She was illiterate, widowed very young, lived on a very limited income, and spoke broken English. Yet she raised five successful children, and remained vital and connected well into her eighties. The size of her funeral — in Mediterranean culture, always a valid standard of measurement — indicated the extent of her impact. She was loved.

Grandma and Grandpa

Chapter Twenty

Dayton Days

My mother and Aunt Martha had come from the Ohio branch of the House of Zennie. The Dayton-Pittsburgh axis was established at a religious pilgrimage. (This is one of those chapters with a lot of exposition, so don't feel guilty if it takes a long time to absorb. This is not, of course, permission to skip it, or even skim it. You may, however, take more time.)

The patron saint of Lebanon is the Blessed Virgin. (I often wonder if this has anything to do with the traditional strength of Lebanese women.) For many years, the Maronite Catholic community in the Northeastern U.S. would go on a pilgrimage over the feast of the Assumption of the Blessed Virgin Mary, which fell on August 15. Each year they would travel to the shrine of Our Lady of Consolation in Carey, Ohio, where they would pray all day and party all night.

Coincidentally (at least I think it was coincidental), my grandmother's birthday fell on August 15. I was about ten or twelve before I realized that all of these people did not show up in her honor. Now that I think about it, my Aunt Gen's birthday fell on August 15 as well. This is getting too complicated; I'm not sure I'm able to plumb its significance.

One year, my father's father and my mother's Aunt Irene, who had known each other in the old country, decided that my father and mother should meet. Since, paradoxically, my mother was old enough to marry, but too young to date, the only result of the introduction was a single meeting each year, at the pilgrimage on the feast of the Assumption.

Eventually, they were permitted to begin dating. This meant that, once or twice a month, on Friday after work, my father would drive to Dayton to court my mother, returning home by Monday morning. In those days before superhighways, it was an eight- or nine-hour trip. That was the beginning.

With my Aunt Martha and Uncle Joe, proximity seemingly bred affection, but World War II intervened. When Joe returned from the Pacific, the plan was that they would marry and live with my parents until Joe completed college.

"So, what's Plan B?"

In addition to Martha, my mother also had three siblings who stayed in Dayton, with whom I was to spend a lot of time over the years. Recovery from rheumatic fever, for me, meant living every summer with my grandparents in Dayton.

It was as if I were leading two or three separate lives. First came my Pittsburgh life, edgy and urban, more streetwise than my parents were really comfortable with, and overlaid with a scarcity of money that helped shape everything.

Then there was my Dayton-Lebanese life, where my grandparents slowly inculcated a set of values, a sensibility, an adapted history, a language, and a cuisine, all based on the Lebanese culture, and all without any formal instruction.

Finally, there was a Dayton-American life, characterized by suburban living and suburban values. Even though I mostly stayed in the city, my aunts and uncles were solidly suburban — middle class — in both values and lifestyle: the burgeoning American Middle Class come to fruition. They provided me with a cumulative total of fifteen first cousins with whom to interact.

My mother's brother Al was a homicide detective. He was an odd blend of the cynic or skeptic and the sentimental family man. I think it showed the contrast between his professional life and his family background. His wife Lila was beautiful, but took no nonsense from anyone.

Aunt Dorothy, in the middle, had insisted on marrying John Thomas, a family cousin, when she was sixteen. The marriage lasted for more than sixty years. Johnny worked at the Inland Steel plant, a subsidiary of one of the major auto companies.

My Uncle Dave, the youngest brother, along with his wife Dolores, formed what I later came to regard as an almost Golden Couple. They both were physically attractive, intelligent, and fun-loving. They seemed to be equal partners at a time when that wasn't common. Dave worked at National Cash Register (NCR), where he had risen remarkably high given that he hadn't completed a college degree. Dolly went back to work when her children were a bit older. She eventually became secretary to one of the generals at Wright-Patterson Air Force Base.

Uncle Dave and Aunt Dolly were usually my first choice when looking for something to do.

My maternal grandfather Joe loved to entertain and enjoyed an active social life. He was an excellent Middle Eastern singer (I am told), and when he was younger, frequently recorded Arabic songs. He also played the Arabic drum called the darbuka.

My memories of him are few, but I always think of him on the days he and his cronies would go out to a local farm to butcher a few lambs for their families. (Every part of the lamb would be utilized, from the legs, which would be served as shish kebab, to the ribs that would be trimmed of meat for stuffing, to the organs — lungs, heart kidneys and liver.) They would return to his house to drink araq and eat some of the lamb. This, inevitably, would take the rest of the day.

He passed away in his early fifties of septicemia caused by a burst appendix. The blood poisoning resulted from following a doctor's admonition to take some Alka Seltzer to settle his stomach.

Ironically, this family tragedy may have saved my life. A few years later, my grandmother was visiting when I developed similar symptoms. My family thought I had simply "eaten something," but my grandmother checked my fever, saw how pale I was, felt my perspiration and insisted that my mother call the doctor. Doctor Kochin left a formal dinner to drive to our house, pick me up, and deliver me to Montefiore Hospital for an emergency appendectomy.

• • •

Since I stayed with my grandparents most of the time I was in Dayton, I was heavily immersed in Lebanese culture and language. Aside from my cousins, my friends were actually my grandparents' friends. My grandmother was famous as a cook and insisted that I learn to prepare Arabic dishes. I had a special bond with her, based on the time I spent with her and the wonderful woman she was.

Norma was the oldest of the grandchildren. She was also the first to move into her own apartment. The fact that it was the remodeled second floor of our grandmother's house was significant for several reasons.

First of all, only a floor apart, we were in frequent contact. Norma projected an image of self-containment. She was a bit wary, as if afraid that someone would try to put something over on her; but she had a wonderful sense of humor and was extremely generous. Although we were born about fifteen years apart, a major difference at that age, we became very close.

Her boyfriend Jack lived across the alley on the next block. He was a long-distance truck driver and was often on the road for several days at a time, followed by several days off. Jack and I took to spending his days off together, while Norma was at work. We would watch the morning quiz shows on TV. We were both fascinated by trivia, and competed to answer the questions before the contestants.

Like Norma, Jack became a good friend. They were adults, and I was a young teenager, but they treated me as a peer. This was one of the relationships in which I didn't feel as if I had to show off to be treated as an adult. They simply accepted me.

They took me everywhere, seldom going on a date without me. I never felt like a third wheel; they made me feel integral to their relationship. Seeing that on paper seems odd. What I really mean to say is that neither Norma nor Jack made me feel anything less than welcome on any occasion.

Tragically, Jack was killed in a car accident shortly after they married.

I developed another special relationship with my cousin Michele. She was one of a set of twins. I hope she will eventually find the grace to forgive me for the following statement: We somehow just seemed to think alike. We were both also possessed of a relatively warped sense of humor, continually laughing at the same — sometimes odd — things. We have remained in contact through all the years, and I still trust her — not a lot of people in that category. I still love her (and her children) in a special way.

And, of course, there was Cousin Gerry, to whom I am forever grateful for teaching me to ride a bike.

My relatives in Dayton were amazingly generous. As a young kid from out of town, with no schedule to maintain and none of my own work to accomplish, I was always free to play. So I would call and say, "Let's do something." It must have taken immense restraint on their part not to brush me off as a royal pain. They never did, that I recall. I was family, and that seemed sufficient to explain and to justify their support.

When I remember Dayton, I also remember places. My memories are defined by Vic Cassano and Mom Denisi's (the pizza parlor where we would order several times a week); the Carillon Bells; the Blue Note, an archetypical neighborhood tavern, and the favorite of my Uncle Al; the recreational facilities provided by the NCR Company, where Aunt Dolly would take us swimming; the NCR Auditorium where we would attend a free movie and get a free candy bar on Saturday mornings. I remember attending movies at the Sigma Movie Theater, and Mass at Emmanuel Church, where you still made an offering at the door, rare in Catholic churches at the time.

The oddest thing I remember about my time in Dayton is discovering trees. In Pittsburgh's Hill District, where I grew up, you had to get on a bus to see a tree. Oh, well, there were stinkweed trees — I believe they were poison sumac — but you never wanted to climb them or even touch them. The smell would linger on your hands.

My grandmother's yard contained a peach tree and two apricot trees, still bearing, and also two large weeping willow trees whose branches, when stripped of leaves, made wonderful whips (I've been told). Those willows fascinated me. They were formidable boundaries in almost any game, and were natural goalposts. Later, in biology class, I was taught that willows grew near a water source. I could never discover that source, unless it was the water well in the next-door neighbor's yard.

To us, my grandmother's yard seemed immense, especially when we had to mow it with a hand mower, and then mow it again when we "missed some spots." Of course, we weren't finished until we used the hand clippers to trim about five miles of fenced borders and decorative wrought-iron fencing.

Although I would never admit it to my siblings, my Dayton relatives spoiled me. I was obviously a center of attention when I was with them. Not only was I "ill." I was alone, living with my grandparents. Furthermore, they knew that my family in Pittsburgh had little money, and I'm sure some of them felt sorry for me.

Eventually, they also realized that being poor deprived us of "things," but not of growth and experiences. Years later, Uncle Dave told me how much he respected my mother and father, that they were able to provide so much for us with so little money.

Back home in Pittsburgh, I led my Pittsburgh life, prowling the urban cityscape at all hours, well, almost all hours.

I enjoyed all three lifestyles.

Joe and Martha and Dave Kail
visit Dayton's Carillon Bells

Chapter Twenty-One

The Great Bicycle Ride

I wasn't supposed to do anything strenuous. After all, I had been ill. I found this to be an excellent principle when applied to a gym excuse. It was less satisfying when applied to my life.

The aftermath of rheumatic fever involved an enlarged heart and some mitral-valve damage. This would ultimately make me 4F for the draft and ineligible to play sports. It was never clear, however, how serious the residual effects were. Was I literally unable to take any type of exercise? Should I just take it easy and avoid anything organized? Could I do some things (e.g., ride a bike, jog, swim) and avoid others (weightlifting, sprints)? Surely some exercise would be good. No one ever told me.

At home, there were enough people around to prevent me from becoming too active. When I visited my relatives in Dayton, they felt sorry for me and weren't so strict.

My grandmother translated all of my limitations into a single rule: I was supposed to take a rest every day. "Taking a rest" meant lying on her couch for about an hour every afternoon. The problem was that this was soap-opera time. She would watch her stories, an assortment of three or four soaps, every afternoon

It was excruciating. It rotted my brain. Occasionally I would hide, hoping my grandmother would forget about the nap. She never did. In fact, if she could discover my hiding place, she was likely to come after me with a broom, shouting through the house as she chased me, "Rest! Rest! You been sick. You gotta rest!"

The trouble was, I didn't feel sick. I felt fine. And I wanted to be as active as any other kid. By this time I was ten or twelve, and I wanted to learn to ride a bike. In Pittsburgh, this was out of the question. We didn't even have bikes. In my neighborhood, bikes were things that you stole from rich kids. In Dayton, my cousin Gerry came to the rescue. Gerry was my Uncle Al's oldest son and was a year younger than I was.

It was a short bus ride to his house from Grandma's, and I was used to riding the bus. When we could, Gerry and I would meet to play together; I would hop on a #8 Ewalt Circle and head out Wyoming Avenue and down Arbor Avenue, their street. We'd usually head for the playground at Cleveland School or walk out Arbor Avenue to the shopping district at Watervliet to check out what was available or what trouble we could get into.

And then Patty got a job. Patty was Al's oldest child, a typical teenager, and she had not so recently discovered boys. That took care of her evenings. Now she had a job, and that meant that her days were accounted for as well. The implications were staggering. She would soon be getting a driver's license — and she no longer needed her bike.

Hers was obviously a girl's bike, with no bar across the center, and a color that looked very feminine, although she denied it. But what did I care? It meant liberty.

With a little help from Gerry, I was on the Freedom Road — not literally, of course, I don't think they had a Freedom Road in Dayton. It meant that I could use Patty's bike to learn to ride. We knew that the adults would frown on our efforts, but Gerry (God bless him!) didn't hesitate for a minute. He began to give me secret bicycle riding lessons.

These lessons consisted of Gerry riding his bike out ahead, and me following, trying to ride without my feet touching the ground every few seconds for balance. Every hundred feet or so, Gerry would patiently stop and wait for me to catch up. This went on for several days. We stayed close to home and would work on my balance and wear out my "tennies." There are those who maintain that I'm still unbalanced (rimshot!).

Finally I managed a thirty- or forty-foot spurt, and we were off. Once I had completed that short distance without falling, or even touching the ground with my feet, longer distances became easy. We began by riding down the alley across the street from Uncle Al's house. It was about three or four hundred feet long and a steep enough grade that you didn't have to pedal; so you could concentrate on your balance. Soon, I was able to ride far enough to get into mischief. And we did. Gerry and I rode all over town, just looking at everything. Since I had some money, we felt free and independent. It was exhilarating.

While my lessons were going on, I did nothing to disabuse my grandmother of the belief that I was riding the bus to Uncle Al's, and Gerry was helping me rest. Once I learned to balance on the two-wheeler, I would figure out how to tell her.

We would've been home free, but Gerry had a faulty sense of direction, so it was his fault when we got lost one day, a short time later. It was to have been our longest ride to date; we were going as far as Grandma's house after lunch to show her that I could ride a bike. I was going to ride so well that she would think that I had always ridden a bike, and wouldn't worry about me "straining" myself. (Ya had to be there.)

I'll never understand how we got so lost.

If you could picture an aerial map of center-city Dayton, Ohio, you would see that the trip was pretty straightforward. All we had to do was to ride two blocks down Arbor Avenue (where Uncle Al's family lived), and make a left onto Wyoming Avenue. Then go straight down Wyoming for two or three miles (past the Blue Note Cafe, Uncle Al's favorite), past Vic Cassano and Mom Denisi's Pizzeria (my favorite), and make a right onto Brown Street. Go past the Sigma Theater, and the firehouse with the koi pond, and in less than a mile we could make another left onto Vine Street, where my grandmother lived. Essentially, it involved three turns and, at most, five miles.

It took us more than four hours.

We rode everywhere in that city. We passed the same buildings two and three times. I'm not sure why we didn't notice turnoffs that we had used before, homes and businesses that we had visited, or landmarks we had explored. Maybe we didn't want to recognize them, or maybe it was a full moon. It would have meant the end of the expedition. Or maybe I was so euphoric at the expertise I had developed on Patty's bike that I wasn't thinking straight.

Whatever the reason, we had left shortly after lunch, and we were now late for dinner. In our family, that was unacceptable. We didn't think to call anyone, and, since we hadn't told anyone our plans, there was no simple explanation. When I didn't turn up at Uncle Al's house for dinner, and Grandma told Uncle Al that we had never appeared at her house, there were some questions to be asked. They had raised too many kids among them to panic, but there was some concern. Al spread the word to his fellow police officers. He asked them to look out for two kids on bikes, and gave out our general descriptions.

By about 6 that evening, we discovered ourselves to be on Burns Avenue, the next block over from Grandma's. We headed home, and were in the final stretch, when we heard a short burst of siren behind us, so we pulled over to the curb. A cop thrust his head out of the driver's window and shouted to us, "You guys belong to Sergeant Zennie?"

That wasn't quite the way I would have expressed it, but we answered, "Yes!"

He said, "Let's go," and tailgated us the remaining distance to 29 Vine Street, Grandma's house.

I'm not sure what the point of this story is, or why I should even worry about a point at this late date. But I do owe Cousin Gerry a vote of thanks for taking the brunt of the reprimand. After all, he was the host. Of course, I wasn't left unscathed. As the older cousin, I should have "known better." Known what better? I was the out-of-towner!

I like to think of this adventure as my "coming out party." Never again did I allow anything except for common sense to prevent me from undertaking a physically demanding project, and, according to my family, I have little common sense.

Years later, during my first year teaching, my mother and father convinced me to invest in a life-insurance policy while I was still young and rates would be more reasonable. They still worried about the remnants of my rheumatic fever.

In discussions with the salesman, he informed me that I had been "rated" by the actuaries, and I would have to pay a higher premium. They had run my numbers and decided that the odds were I wouldn't live beyond my fifty-first birthday.

I knew that was a sucker's bet. After all, I had survived the Great Bicycle Ride — and its aftermath. I was going to make them look silly.

And I did.

Chapter Twenty-Two

Poison Okra

I t all started because we were lazy. I'm sure we would have had a different explanation at the time, but, at root, we were being lazy.

We woke up one weekday morning at my grandmother's house on Vine Street in Dayton, Ohio. Bob and Dick, my older brothers, and I were there for two weeks pursuing what passed for a vacation in our household, i.e., two weeks at Grandma's.

Our presence had been announced by our photos on her dining room buffet. This was a method we developed as young kids. My grandmother had twenty-five grandchildren and at least twenty-five great-grandchildren, each of whom would provide her with the requisite school photo every year. She would feature all of them on the buffet until it became impractical to show all of them at once. She then adopted a loose rule to control the flow.

Grandma would feature your grade-school graduation photo, your high-school graduation photo, and your wedding photo. They would be displayed for a year, and then would be placed in the top buffet drawer to make room for the next batch. Once we realized that she kept all of these photos in the drawer, it was a short leap to our signal system. When we were in town, we would simply search out our photos and place them in the middle of all the others. That way, if our relatives stopped by, they would know immediately that the Kail hordes had descended.

If I remember correctly, this was the same summer Dick fell in love for almost the entire two weeks with Louise, the daughter of a family friend. In those days, without either money or a car, it was difficult to initiate, let alone sustain, a romance. But Dick was determined, and hinted at success.

We tended to get up early when we stayed at my grandmother's; of course, our idea of early and her idea differed by at least an hour. Grandma rousted us out of bed that day, because we were going over to "Uncle Richard's" to work in the garden. Richard was Aunt Nouf's son. Nouf was one of my grandmother's best friends — the "Aunt" was an honorific — and her daughter Dolores was married to my Uncle Dave. Both families were of the House of Zennie, although Nouf spelled it "Zenni," I believe. Richard was also brother to my Aunt Dolores. Do you have all that straight?

This project was disconcerting on several levels. First of all, we had to get out of bed early; we were actually up and dressed before nine. Second, this meant we were going to spend most of the day with Grandma and Aunt Nouf, two loving and kind older women, and wonderful cooks, but not necessarily scintillating conversationalists.

Finally, we were going to have to do actual work. This wasn't showcase effort to impress the relatives with our work ethic and our industriousness; this was actual work, where you might sweat.

Now, before you go patronizing us and ridiculing our definition of labor, remember that we were on a two-week vacation, and looking forward to doing nothing here in Ohio.

I don't remember how we got to Richard's house, since neither of the two women drove a car. When we arrived, however, they told us to weed the large garden in the rear, while they did some laundry and general cleaning ("… And be careful of the tomatoes").

Richard was seldom around, and no one ever explained his frequent absences. There were hints of "drinking" and other rumors, but they were never fully developed. There were whispers about "the War" and living in Hawaii, among other obscure references, but I don't think I had seen Richard more than twice in my life. In both instances, he seemed like a nice guy.

It was puzzling to us that he had a house in Dayton, since he was seldom there, and we weren't quite clear about who kept up the house while he was gone. Nor did it seem we were going to find out.

In other words, he was a complete mystery to us.

So, we went around to this enormous garden in back of the house to begin our adventures with the soil. It was vast; it looked like the Western prairie or a Russian Steppe. It was the vegetable equivalent of Noah's Ark, with representatives of every conceivable form of vegetation.

And we had to weed it.

That seems like a simple task, limited only by our energy and commitment. But we had grown up in the city; actually, in a very questionable part of the city. We didn't know a tomato plant from Jack's Beanstalk, or a willow from a weed.

So we attacked the garden, laying waste to vegetation in the attempt to eliminate weeds. Soon we were sweating, nettles clinging to our clothes, dirt streaking our necks and torsos, hands red from toil. We felt proud, back to the soil, in touch with our primordial personae. This was hard work. We looked at a watch. We had been weeding for twenty-five minutes.

We were on vacation; we shouldn't have to do forced manual labor. We put out heads to the task and came up with an approach that we were sure would not only provide respite, but also sympathy. We were going to flimflam the old women. I'm not sure, in the final analysis, whose idea it was, but we piled on a bit more dirt and went running into the house shouting. "Grandma, Grandma, we fell in the Poison Okra! It got all over us."

How we came up with the "poison okra" I'll never know. Why not poison oak or poison ivy? I guess it just seemed more impressive and dangerous.

And that's when the fun began.

Grandma and Aunt Nouf gathered around us making sympathetic noises. We thought we would probably have to take a shower and then we would be free of our onerous responsibilities.

Boy, did we get it wrong.

They pointed us toward the shower all right, but that's where standard operating procedure vanished and we entered terra incognita. We were sent to the basement shower. When we got downstairs, the first thing they did was to strip us bare naked, and then throw our clothes into the washing machine. Since we had no spare clothing, this sort of committed us to nudity. It was embarrassing.

We thought the next move would be — finally — to take a shower, but that wasn't good enough for Grandma and Nouf. Never let it be said that they were less than thorough. Instead of standing us under the showerhead and letting us wash off the deadly poison okra, they did us one better.

They stood us up in two large galvanized washtubs and sprayed us with cold water from the hose. It was freezing, but that wasn't the end of our ignominy. To be safe, they began to scrub us down with old-fashioned laundry soap and stiff scrub brushes, removing several layers of skin in their determination to defeat the impact of that deadly vegetation. And when I say they scrubbed us down, I mean all of us, not a fleshly nook or cranny escaped their ministrations.

I'm not sure how it feels to be flogged or flayed, or maybe to be attacked by jellyfish with their stingers. It could not, however, have been much worse than what we experienced. We were further humiliated because we weren't sure whether these wily old crones understood our ploy completely and were teaching us a lesson, or they were kind and innocent and doing what they could to relieve our symptoms based on their best knowledge. To this day, I'm not sure who was flimmed and who was flammed, and, of course, they did nothing to relieve our ignorance.

Later, I heard the two of them laughing in the kitchen. I have no evidence as to the cause of their laughter; it may have been totally innocent. I didn't really want to know. You will never convince me, however, that they were not laughing at us and our pitiable big-city ploy to get out of working.

Chapter Twenty-Three

The New Ford Fairlane

S everal sets of circumstances combined to create this dark moment in my personal biography. First of all, money was tight. Reasons ranged from urban renewal to bad luck to a large family. But poor people know you never need an explanation for poverty. My father had bought only one new car since before the war, a 1952 Chevrolet station wagon; at least, I think it was new. For the most part, he simply developed a close relationship with a long line of cheap clunkers.

But now he had a brand new Ford Fairlane.

It was the cheapest and most basic model. It had no radio. In retrospect, I'm not even sure it had a heater. We named it "Congress," because it never passed anything. But it was a new Ford Fairlane.

The second of the intersecting sets of circumstances centered on the fact that I had just had my sixteenth birthday the month before. In American society at that time, that also meant that I could apply for my driver's license, which I did. Finally, there was my matriculation at Central Catholic High School, with all that implied; among the implications being strong friendships and an active sports program. Nobody who attended either school would dare to miss the annual Central Catholic/North Catholic football game.

I asked for the car.

It would be the first time I would take it out alone. There was an immediate and unanimous uproar. "Don't give him the car, he's too young!" and "Not for a football game! He's only had his license for a week." and "He just wants to drive around and pick up girls!"

Well, I was sixteen. Of course I wanted to drive around and pick up girls.

My dad, normally conventional, but with a strong streak of independence, told them all to back off. He was going to allow me to take a giant step toward self-realization; he was giving me the car for the game.

Understand what this involved. I did not simply get the keys and drive away on game night. My father would drive to the night shift at our family tavern in the Uptown area. (The kindest thing that could be said about the neighborhood was that it was in a "transitional" stage.) At the appropriate time, I would have to take the bus down Fifth Avenue, resplendent in my cheerleader's uniform, pick up the car, return it after the game, and take a bus home.

The Complications

For the first time in several years, we won the game. Make that "WE WON THE GAME!" At least that's how everyone felt. And we all headed back to Central to celebrate by ringing the Victory Bell.

(For those of you who count yourselves among the younger generations of the family, please don't judge us harshly. It was a simpler time.)

It was difficult to find a space in the parking lot. Finally, I spied a spot in the corner of the lot. Two cars were parked at a ninety-degree angle, and I was able to slip between them on the diagonal.

We celebrated the victory.

When I returned to the car to leave, I assumed that I was flanked by the same two cars, giving me three or four inches of clearance on each side.

I was wrong.

The car on the driver's side had been replaced by another car. It provided no clearance.

As I backed up, I scraped the whole driver's side from front fender to back door. It would have been worse, but I finally realized what had happened and stopped. Nevertheless, I had scraped my father's one-week-old new Ford Fairlane.

Everyone expressed sympathy, even the driver of the other car. But they didn't understand. I had scraped my father's one-week-old new Ford Fairlane. How do you apologize for that? How do you apologize for betraying a father's trust? For repaying his faith with a stripe on the fender?

I drove the car slowly back to the bar and parked it. I debated with myself, but it was self-deception. I knew I didn't have the guts to go into the bar and stand in front of my father's regulars and tell him/them about the car. So I got on a bus and went home to wait for my father.

The Dénouement

I sat in the living room with my face in my hands and waited from 1:30 until 4 a.m., exploring all options. There were none.

Finally, the key turned in the door and I heard my father enter. He took forever to cover the four feet from the front door to the living room. I stood up to prepare myself. The words were like acid in my mouth: "Dad, I am so sorry!"

I never got to say them.

Instead, my father looked at me and said, "Do you know what happened to the car?"

I tried again to speak, unsuccessfully.

He interrupted me again. "Some drunken S.O.B. in a big Cadillac smacked the car, knocked it over the curb and into a wall. It's scraped all along both sides."

I positively leaped to my feet and shouted, "Oh, damn!"

The unutterable sense of relief I felt was immediately followed by the pangs of a moral dilemma. I solved it.

I waited for five years to tell him.

Chapter Twenty-Four

Pound Cake and Nut Horns

T he family bar — known legally at various points as either the S&K or the A.H.P. — was usually simply called "Dave's place" or "Dave and Helen's." This reflected the fact that it was more than a bar; it was part of the social structure, part of the neighborhood. It functioned almost as a safety zone.

Despite the questionable nature of the area, Dave and Helen's was as close as you could come in that area to being a neighborhood tavern. It had implied rules (e.g., no drug deals), a code of behavior (you take care of each other when necessary and possible), and a pool of regular customers. One of the regulars was the head baker at a kosher bakery in the area.

I'm not sure whether my father had done him a major favor, or it was in return for spirits rendered, but for many years at about 9 p.m. on Sunday evening — every Sunday evening — the baker would drop off at the house two large bakery bags filled with baked goods straight from the oven. The one bag contained rye bread and pumpernickel loaves that were still warm. The house smelled heavenly.

The other bag was filled with pound cakes and pastries, goodies such as nut horns, cinnamon-raisin rolls, and elephant ears. (If you don't recognize these delicacies, your culinary life is incomplete.)

And that forms the heart of this story, every week for more than ten years we received two large bags filled with baked goods straight from the oven.

The bread took care of itself; it was always needed for sandwiches or toast, or butter and jelly. Actually, much of it never survived beyond Sunday night. We would grab the hot bread at the door, run with it to the kitchen smelling the fragrance from the bag, tear off a chunk, slather it with butter, and wallow in the endorphins it engendered.

The pastries were something different. We all had a sweet tooth, but you can only eat so many nut horns and raisin rolls. At some point you wanted a pie.

And the pound cake … It was wonderful! Good as it was, however, you could only eat so much pound cake. My Aunt Martha took to disguising it. We had toasted pound cake, toasted pound cake with butter and jelly, pound cake with various syrups, pound cake with strawberries and whipped cream, pound cake with pudding or ice cream. But again, at some point you wanted a cookie.

As the pound-cake supply line continued to operate, but the pound cake consumption rate declined, we devised a stopgap solution. We began to store the pound cakes in an old Coldspot twenty-seven-cubic-foot chest freezer in the basement. This solution, however, was inherently temporary; there was only room for about two- or three hundred cakes. We eventually hit upon a more permanent solution. Pound cakes, especially of this quality, made wonderful gifts.

They also made wonderful breakfasts. At this time, I was still serving the 2:30 Mass every Sunday morning. If I were at a party — or, more likely, running in a show — I would usually end the night dragging a few friends to 2:30 Mass. The reward for such orthodoxy was breakfast at the Kail house after Mass, usually featuring pound cake and coffee. The guests inevitably commented on the high quality of the pound cake, providing an opening for a gift. We were usually successful at providing a pound cake for each hand.

Several impecunious local actors made it through some rough times on the breakfasts and pound cakes from the Kails.

It always interested me how accepting my friends and family were of each other. If one of my siblings, in a ratty bathrobe, encountered one of my friends, in sweaty work clothes and in need of a shower, eating breakfast in the kitchen at some ungodly hour of the morning, neither would be fazed. He or she would automatically assume it was one of my friends and say good morning. This made for excellent relationships but horrible hygiene.

To this day, many of my oldest friends comment fondly on those breakfasts and those pound cakes. In retrospect, it's amazing how much they have grown in size and quality.

Florida Forensics Trip

Chapter Twenty-Five

The Gym Excuse

I have said elsewhere that many of my siblings thought I was spoiled when I was growing up. My childhood bout with rheumatic fever caused me to receive special treatment. For the most part, they were probably right. I can't quite quantify it, or even describe it; but there were subtle differences in our treatment by our parents that, I'm sure, caused the belief that I was spoiled.

On the other hand, they weren't even aware of some of the things I had to go through because of the residual heart problems that circumscribed my activities. For example, I was not allowed to play organized sports. That was a no-brainer. The standard wisdom was that my heart couldn't take the intense training programs.

My solution was to play disorganized sports. The games I played were the equivalent of a second- or third-string gathering of the geeks. I'm not sure why the other kids were there, but I was pretty sure it had to do with a lack of talent. At this level of competition, I was above average.

The problem was that we had last claim on any facilities we wanted to use, the sandlot, the gym, the parking lot, and so on. I suppose we should have been pleased that we weren't bullied very often — we were prime candidates — but, for some reason, the older/stronger guys in the neighborhood left us pretty much alone. It might have had something to do with the fact that all of us had older brothers; most of us had several.

The ban on strenuous activities extended to simpler things, such as running (not to be thought of), climbing stairs (to be strictly limited), riding bikes (not permitted), swimming (a rest every fifteen minutes), and fighting (no problem). Every parent in the whole neighborhood was aware of the strictures on my activities, and felt that they were contributing to neighborhood harmony if they prevented me from doing anything at all. I really had to struggle to experience any of the typical activities of childhood that formed most kids.

And it continued as I attended high school. Up until that point, very few people outside the family or neighborhood were told of my imposed physical limitations, but they became painfully obvious in gym class. This occurred for several reasons. First of all, I was not permitted to take an extra course, or even a study period, in place of gym. In a burst of creative bureaucracy, the school required me to show up at gym class twice a week for two years.

The gym teacher made it painfully obvious he felt that I was goldbricking; I couldn't possibly be sick for two whole years. He wouldn't let me leave for the library or a study hall. For each of those years, before each gym class, he would demand I show up and provide my written gym excuse. Once during the second semester of my sophomore year, I misplaced it. The gym teacher made sure to shortstop a reign of chaos and anarchy by sending me to detention (as if he didn't know!).

Luckily, when I traveled to Dayton to visit my mother's family, while they were apprised of the ban on strenuous physical activity, it was honored more in the breach. Of course my grandmother had a whole collection of spoken admonitions — "Rest, Honey, rest!" and "Don't run!" — but she seldom followed up on an active level. Thus, my Uncle Dave frequently took me swimming at his company's pool, and my cousin Gerry taught me to ride a bike.

All of this de-emphasis on physical activity had an obvious counterbalance in the life of the mind. All four parents in the house were voracious readers. My father and Aunt Martha tended toward fiction, especially mysteries, while my mother and Uncle Joe preferred news and nonfiction. I learned to read very young, and became voracious myself, starting from comic books and progressing through children's novels, and into standard novels. Typically, I spent hours at the main branch of Carnegie Library and Museum, both of which were excellent.

It also became clear that I was not going to be a wrestler or a linebacker. My family encouraged me to think in terms of more sedentary pursuits. Dr. Kochin, my pediatrician, suggested that I think about the priesthood, so that I could plan on an easy life. Personally, I wanted to be a cowboy, but given the cruel circumstances — i.e., I had no cows — I began to think of becoming a teacher. That, however, was in the future.

The theme of physical limitation and its interface with bureaucracy reared its ugly head once again when I attended college. Since it was a Land Grant college, all males attending Duquesne University were required to take ROTC training. Only physical disability could excuse you. My doctor wrote a letter for each of the two required years, explaining that my physical limitations would prohibit participation in the Armed Forces. I would be 4F in the draft.

Two weeks before graduating from college, I received a registered letter informing me that, since I had never taken ROTC, I would not be permitted to graduate.

My first reaction was disbelief. My second was anger. I had complied with the rules and had submitted a letter from my doctor for each of the two years it was required. It wasn't my fault if the idiots had misplaced them.

Remember, ROTC was only required for two years. I had been attending Duquesne for four years. This, of course, meant that these idiots had two years to discover that I had not attended any ROTC classes and notify me of the possible consequences. I was even more upset when I contemplated whether it was intentional.

I wouldn't actually have minded if I couldn't clear up the situation until after commencement. I wouldn't really miss the graduation procession and ceremonies. But it turned out that my father, who had never attended any activity I had been involved with — not a play, not a debate tournament, not an honors convocation, not a public presentation of any type — had decided to attend his son's commencement. I was stuck. I had to fight the good fight.

I began making the rounds of the power structure to see what could be done. I visited my advisor, the dean of the School of Education, the chair of the English Department, and the dean of studies. They all seemed sympathetic, but unable to do anything. A couple of them even gave an uncomfortable smile.

ROTC was the only program that could prevent graduation. The dean of studies could modify the requirements of other departments.

The requirements of the ROTC program, however, were sacrosanct.

I finally discovered that only the ROTC commanding colonel could dispense me from the ROTC requirement. When I attempted to call him, I was informed that he was on vacation with his family. I returned for a second round of pleading visits to the advisor, the dean, the chair, and the dean, and once again the bottom line was a series of uncomfortable smiles followed by inaction.

I finally persuaded one of the younger ROTC officers to find out where the colonel was vacationing, contact him, verify that I had followed the proper procedure of providing a physician's notice of disability, and have the colonel send a telegram releasing me from the military training requirement. This arrived two days before commencement.

I found out the reason that everyone was so uncomfortable during my appointments to plead for action. I was to receive the Outstanding Graduate Award. They were smiling at the irony, convinced that someone would do something. Of course that someone ended up being me.

My father waited to hear my name announced from the stage, and then got up, left the auditorium, and went home.

It's hard to describe the effect of being told over and over that physical exertion was dangerous. Not knowing the extent of the damage from the rheumatic fever, almost anything physical could be considered deadly, although I guess that's a bit dramatic. As an adult, I might have thought to do some research, or at least I could have made a conscious decision how far I would go. But, no one ever explained my condition to me. I was simply a kid who had been told, basically, that any time I did something that caused me to breathe heavily, I could end up dead.

Through all that time, there was no way to develop a sense of perspective. As a child there was no one to talk to, even if I could articulate the fears. And by the time I grew up, I was set in my ways.

I guess I'm glad that all of this happened when I was young. It's impossible for a kid to bear these kinds of weighty warnings unremittingly over the years. He's bound to forget about it and simply begin to take the risks of living as full a life as possible. And I did.

Chapter Twenty-Six

My First Apartment

It was simple. You lived at home until you married, then you were permitted (but not required) to establish your own home with your spouse. This wasn't just orthodoxy, this was family scripture. This was the way it was.

And then my brother Bob — who had entered the seminary and left before ordination, who had to start over completely but managed to squeeze a college education into four or five years while teaching full-time, who was the favorite son — moved away from home. My parents were not pleased, but they didn't really have a choice. It was Bob, and it was a fait accompli.

I was perfectly content to remain at home. I had started a job as a teacher in a Catholic high school. I was in graduate school, and I was doing a lot of theatre. What I wasn't doing was earning much money. Staying at home meant I didn't have to worry about maintaining an apartment. And the pittance I paid my parents for rent helped pull them out of a financial hole.

But they were not going to be caught flatfooted again. Some type of (unreliable) family radar gave them hints about when I was contemplating getting an apartment. I never contemplated getting an apartment until I did, but for several years my parents waged a subtle campaign.

Any time they thought, for whatever reason, that I was considering flight, they would launch a low-level attack. They would, however subtly, find ways to illustrate what I would be missing by moving.

Sometimes it was simply the fact that my favorite foods would appear more frequently on the menu. Sometimes I would find a candy bar on my pillow, or my father would stop after closing his bar and bring me a sundae from the all-night drugstore. Once, I came home and discovered that a TV had appeared in my bedroom.

I never knew what precipitated the latest campaign, or why they didn't just ask. I think it had something to do with a sort of family code. My family seldom discussed things that were deeply significant. Of course, we all talked about things, even some important things. But meaningful, soul-baring discussions or insights were infrequent at best. We all assumed a lot. By osmosis, or some other more mystical process, we would somehow come to understand the situation and act appropriately. Actually, the system worked fairly well.

I think some of it had to do with my dad's deafness. A victim of scarlet fever in his youth, he became progressively more hard of hearing. It was difficult to carry on any lengthy discussion, and it would have to take place at a high decibel level, not exactly conducive to heartfelt conversations.

It was literally years before I learned to be comfortable having a conversation with the family that really mattered, and even then only with two of my brothers and one or two sister/cousins. And eventually I was blessed with the ability to share somewhat with my then-octogenarian Aunt Martha, one of the four household parents.

Getting back to the apartment saga, when I was in my late twenties, I was offered the opportunity to take over the lease of a friend who was moving to Japan. It was a great apartment, in the heart of a hot area of the city, with reasonable rent. I couldn't say no. But I thought long and hard over how to tell my parents. Eventually I asked my two older brothers for some help, and they stopped by to help break the news.

I wrote my parents a long letter explaining that, by leaving, I wasn't rejecting them or their values. I was simply moving. I had great respect for how they had raised us and what they taught us, especially by example.

I know my mother cried, and I suspect my father did as well; but they came to accept it. Years later, when we were cleaning out my mother's papers after her death, I found the letter folded up and tucked into a corner of a drawer. At that point, I cried.

I later found that, while my mother's angst had to do with the nature of family and relationships; some of Dad's upset about my move distilled itself into concern about my lack of mechanical ability. He was afraid I couldn't take care of my car. He had worked as a machinist for many years, but felt he hadn't passed on his mechanical inclination to any of his sons.

His solution, when he thought my car was due for inspection, was to drive to my apartment after closing the bar, leave his car wherever he could find a parking space — always a challenge in Shadyside — and take my car to be serviced. When I awoke and left for work, I had to remember where I had parked my car; and, if it wasn't there, look around for his car in order to make some kind of determination as to whether mine had been stolen or was simply being serviced.

His concern about my lack of mechanical ability was well founded but not really relevant. After all, I had learned some basic carpentry and painting skills by building stage sets. One such episode occurred during the Christmas season. My response to my parents' inevitable question — i.e., "What do you want for Christmas?" — was usually, "Nothing, I don't need anything."

That year, caught up in building a massive set for a large musical, I replied, "I could use a power drill." My father got so excited that any of his sons was doing something mechanical that he provided a whole toolbox of equipment, including a jigsaw, a ripsaw, and a drill. I was the fair-haired son for almost a week.

There are a number of ancillary stories branching from the apartment saga. The first has to do with moving day, which was accomplished with two friends and a VW Microbus. With the final load, my mother handed me two brown cardboard boxes, saying "You'll probably want these later."

As we unpacked the last busload, I grabbed the boxes and stuck them in a closet. After a few weeks, as I was finishing the unpacking, I found them and opened them.

In the top box was every towel, ashtray, knife, fork, napkin and washcloth I had ever stolen from a hotel on what was a pretty extensive travel schedule. My mother's sense of morality would not permit her to use them in the family house, but it seems it was OK for me to use them to start my solo life.

The other box contained the program, ticket, and review from every theatre performance I had ever done. Since I seldom read reviews until after a show, and they were frequently gone by then, I had actually never read many of those in the box. It was a touching gesture.

Since my father had never seen me in a play — primarily due to his growing deafness and working the night shift at the bar — I assumed that my mother had clipped and saved everything. She informed me that it was my dad, that he had done it for years. That made it even more touching. (Of course, we didn't discuss it. I simply said thanks.)

A whole series of tales are caught up in furnishing my apartment, since I had little money. I bought the couch and chair from Harry, the former tenant. They were made out of the universal sculpted green fabric (I think it was related to Brillo). One rear leg sat on two bricks. My end tables consisted of one beer case and one single drawer file cabinet — each covered with linoleum. I had a bed, a chest of drawers, an easy chair, and a dining room table that, since the 1930s, had held up cases of beer in the basement of my father's bar. When I invited people to dinner, and they asked if they could bring anything, I usually responded, "Chairs!"

What I thought to be my most innovative adaptation turned out to be a fiasco. My single credit card being maxed out well before all of the incidentals were purchased, I often found myself in a "make-do" mode. Luckily, I had also received the ancient curtains on the various windows from Harry, but this didn't include the rather important bathroom window. This remained bare. My ingenious (I thought) solution was to go to the dollar store, and spend a dollar for some cheap plastic curtains complete with valence.

When I got them home and went to hang them, I found the dimensions — 60x72" — applied in the direction opposite the one I assumed, and the 60" didn't reach the bottom of the window. But I was still in the creative mode! I quickly grabbed a stapler, and reversing the curtains, I stapled the curtains to the bottom of the plastic valence getting an extra twelve of bottom coverage. Ta-da!

No one ever noticed the difference.

Except for Bob.

He noticed everything.

And since he was Bob, he took great delight in pointing it out to my mother. She was so upset that she insisted on buying bathroom curtains herself.

This, of course, fostered a dilemma. In justice, I should have created havoc somewhere in Bob's life, just to get even.

On the other hand, I had new bathroom curtains.

Still another story involves a phone call I received from my sister/cousin Patty, the youngest sibling. She had been living in Baltimore, but had just gotten a job in Pittsburgh and was returning home. Knowing how hard it would be to live at the family house after being on her own for so long, she asked if she could stay at my place until she found an apartment. I agreed.

When word reached "the house" (which, to this day, is how we refer to where we all grew up), we were quickly and forcefully informed that she would be living at home. I guess acceptance of my move didn't extend to the girls of the house.

Chapter Twenty-Seven

First Loves

In contemporary America, we are more likely to discuss our love life than our economic life. I think that tendency is ass-backwards. How did the economics of everyday living become more personal than one's love life?

My own love life has always been just that, my love life. There are few people with whom I would discuss it. This chapter, therefore, may cause some interest among those who think I'm a womanizer and those who think I'm gay. Those who couldn't care less, however, I'm pretty sure, comprise the largest category by far. They are permitted to skip this confessional exercise.

We had always brought our friends home, and I continued the tradition for as long as I lived at the house. You were welcome to meet my friends, but I never considered my relationships appropriate topics for discussion or gossip. They were what they were and what we made them.

Why was it anyone's concern whether my relationship with a woman involved a sexual aspect? I came bitterly to resent those who would ask, "Is she your girlfriend or just a friend?" Just a friend. In my mind, that linguistic usage signified the smallness of the person who would use it. In the Kail world that was entirely reasonable. In the real world, people sometimes thought I must have something to hide.

I dated regularly throughout high school, and my dates tended to be friends as well as dates, but I never went steady. This meant that my friends considered me available when their girlfriend's best friend needed a date to the prom or whatever. When my relatives and friends stop by my house today, they sometimes love to spend time looking at the prom pictures I could never bring myself to throw away, and laughing like hell at their old-fashioned formality.

My first real love was Mary K. She always felt that "Mary" was too plain a name, so we all called her Mary K. Mary K was from Dayton, Ohio, and that's where the fun begins.

By the time I was in college, I no longer spent whole summers in Dayton, but I would drive down several times a year to see my grandmother and other relatives. I would usually take a nap, get up about midnight or 1 a.m., and leave in the very early morning. If traffic broke properly, I would arrive in Dayton at about 6 or 7 a.m., just in time to stop and have breakfast with Uncle Dave and Aunt Dolly, whose house was on the way. I would then head for my grandmother's.

I was down in Dayton for a weekend, right after my high-school graduation, when Uncle Al and Aunt Lila invited me over for dinner. I didn't usually wait for an invitation, but this time they obviously had something in mind.

During dinner, Uncle Al looked at me and started.

"Do you have a girlfriend?" he asked. "Y'know, Judge Fox's daughter is going to school in Pittsburgh; you should look her up. You'll like her, she's a nice kid, and she's cute."

"Who's Judge Fox?"

"He's just a local judge."

"How do you know she's cute? Have you met her?" Knowing my uncle, it was all based on geography: she happened to be in Pittsburgh, and he was in Dayton with Judge Fox.

"This isn't a debate, Eugene." He still called me Eugene, not Gene, placing the stress on the first syllable. "Her dad told me she was pretty. You should look her up. Her name is Mary."

I filed the whole exchange under "F" for "Forget this," and returned to Pittsburgh where I had a summer job.

At the end of the summer following my freshman year at Duquesne, I was in Ohio again. I was with Uncle Dave and Aunt Dolly when they began talking about plans for the "International Affair." That was their local folk festival, and they were chairing it that year. My Aunt Dolly had quite a reputation as a Middle-Eastern dancer and teacher.

They thought they were being subtle, but it was clear they had rehearsed the next part of the conversation.

147

Aunt Dolly: "I don't know if we told you, but there was a really nice girl, who was working with us on the Affair, who goes to school in Pittsburgh."

Uncle Dave: "Yeah, she dances with the Tamburitzans. Aren't they at Duquesne?"

He disingenuously referred to the world-famous ethnic song and dance troupe that was headquartered at Duquesne University.

I said, "yes" to the Tamburitzan question and in my head said "no" to the implied question. While I trusted Dave and Dolly, I had been burned too many times. Once again I returned to Pittsburgh, where I started my sophomore year at Duquesne.

Skip to Veteran's Day. I think every college in the country has a policy, written or not, that states if a teacher is late for a class by ten minutes or more, the class can leave. Some schools refine it further: If the teacher holds a doctorate, or is a full professor, you have to wait for twenty minutes before leaving. When Dr. Hugo didn't show up for our 11 a.m. Anthropology class that November 11, we split the difference. At 11:15 I stood up and said, "Hey, I'm going down to the Veteran's Day Parade, anyone interested?" I loved parades.

Several of the other students joined me and we walked down the hill to the parade site on Fifth Avenue.

Over the next couple of hours, I began talking to a girl from class who was standing next to me. She was cute and seemed intelligent, at least she was smart enough to laugh at my jokes. When I asked her name, she replied it was Mary K, which I thought was Mary Kay (like the make-up.) She then asked mine, and I said it was Gene.

This can get a bit confusing. All of my life, all of my family called me either Eugene (first syllable stress) or Euge (rhymes with "huge"). In high school, however, all of my friends began to call me Gene. The family later learned to call me Gene, but never with a great deal of ease. Until the day she died, you could hear the slight hitch in my mother's voice just before she called me "Gene."

So we were Gene and Mary Kay, not Eugene and Mary. I asked her out.

We were having midterm exams, so we didn't get very far into the relationship. We were both on scholarship and put in long hours of study. Over the next couple of weeks we probably talked on the phone a few times and might possibly have gone to a movie.

Sitting in class later in November, I happened to glance at her hand, and noticed a school ring from Julienne High School.

"Hey, some of my relatives went to a Julienne High School, but it was in Dayton, Ohio."

Her face told me all I needed to know. Like me, she had taken her father's comment, "You should look him up," with a grain of salt. Like me she had carefully smiled and forgotten about it. Like me, she was now stuck. If we told our respective families that we were dating, they would have us married within the year — or nag for years afterward about missed opportunities.

We didn't tell them we were dating until several months later, especially not Uncle Al, Aunt Lila, Uncle Dave, and Aunt Dolly. We risked their displeasure, to put it mildly. I can't tell you how much they cherished the opportunity to say, "I told you so!"

With a houseful of kids, it was difficult to study in the evenings, so I often took a short nap in the afternoon and studied late at night, sometimes not going to bed again until 3 or 4 a.m. This schedule worked well for me, because it also facilitated late-night rehearsals or theatre performances.

The fact that I kept such odd hours also simplified the relationship with Mary K. She would often return very late to the dorms after a presentation with the Tamburitzans, who performed all over the world. I would meet the bus, help unload the costumes and instruments, and then she and I would head somewhere for food or coffee.

Sometimes we went to the house, and she would be there when everyone awoke. They would matter-of-factly share breakfast with her and head off to school. My family seemed to like her, which was not always a given, even before they knew she was the "Dayton connection." But I could tell that Aunt Martha had reservations. It took a while, but I finally got it out of her. Mary K was always moving; she could never sit still. She made Aunt Martha nervous.

We didn't discuss it much — probably my fault — but we pretty much agreed that, while we cared very much, and there was a strong connection, she was a dancer. Her career was not going to be in Pittsburgh. And I wasn't prepared to follow her wherever her career would take her. After college, she headed out to California to work on a master's in dance at UCLA.

She became a ballerina, and eventually taught ballet at the Boston Conservatory. We kept in touch off and on over the years. Several of the young actors with whom I worked in Pittsburgh later studied at the Conservatory, and they would pass greetings back and forth.

The pattern repeated itself years later with Koni, a wonderful actress, originally from Pittsburgh, who simply came home for a while and then headed for California. The same affection, the same connection, the same result.

There were several others, wonderful women who deserved more of me than I was prepared to give.

When several "serious" relationships ended the same way, although not for the same reasons, it became clear that I was the problem. The armchair psychologist would probably maintain that I had a pronounced fear of intimacy and an obvious lack of willingness to commit. And the armchair psychologist would probably be right. (I hate it when that happens.) I guess I still do have those qualities. But they're simply a description, not an explanation, or an analysis.

This seems to be a characteristic of the Kail men. We often have a problem with intimacy. It is difficult to find someone with whom we can allow ourselves to become vulnerable.

I'm not sure why. I've thought a lot about it over the years. I know it's a bit late, but I am trying to learn now. I hope I have enough time.

Mary K

Chapter Twenty-Eight

The Game of Categories

My mother placed us in categories. She made judgments concerning our tastes, interests, and activities, the basis for which continually eluded us. This played out in many ways.

For example, in Mom's mind, I was the smart one (though I lacked common sense). Dick was the businessman; he oozed common sense and practicality. Bob was the nurturing one. Ironic, because I was the one who ran my own business for twenty years; Dick was the only one of us who married and reproduced; and Bob was the Associate Dean of Engineering at a distinguished American university for more than two decades.

While she would never admit it, we all knew that Bob was Mom's favorite. The signs were subtle, but present. For instance, she was more likely to talk to Bob when she was worried.

Dick felt he was my father's favorite, but I knew I was. Far from being grounds for controversy or jealousy, we often teased them and each other, just to hear them deny they had any favorites.

Mom didn't drive; she depended on Dad, and then us "kids," to get done what she needed to get done. This was no real handicap; typically, she would be driven where she wanted to go, when she wanted to go there. I never heard her express the need for a driver's license.

Her travel schedule, however, was based neither on happenstance nor whimsy. Rather, it was based on availability, our availability. Over the years, she had developed a very clear picture in her mind about which of us was capable and willing to perform which tasks for her, especially after my father passed away and she took over management of the family tavern.

Bob took her shopping, whether for clothes or for food. It was Dick's task to review any contract, insurance form, or business decision. I was arm candy. Somehow my brothers had convinced her that I loved escorting her to family gatherings such as weddings, parties, and funerals. This not only released them from what they considered an onerous task; it also served to remind me that I was both the youngest and the least. You can bet they loved that.

One day Dick and I were at the house, sitting in the kitchen talking, drinking coffee, and stripping Mom's larder of anything edible. Mom stuck her head in the kitchen door and asked, "Do you know if Bob is coming over today. I need to go to the Giant Eagle."

Dick and I just looked at each other; we had obviously failed some subtle supermarket test. To this day we are not sure how or why she arrived at the conclusions she did.

• • •

I am a single uncle with a large family and a large number of friends. People buy me things. I have also had several friends who are artists, and whenever I could afford it, I would buy one of their works. I try not to clutter up my house with tchotchkes; most of the decorative elements are either gifts or works by artist acquaintances. I could never afford a house large enough to display the large number of beautiful and generous gifts I have received over the years. I hate to have beautiful things sit in a drawer. They ought to be displayed and admired and used.

OK, the secret is now out. I confess I am also an inveterate re-gifter. I feel if I enjoyed someone's gift, I can double the joy by passing it on to another friend for whom it would be appropriate.

One year I got the bright idea to re-gift on a major scale. At the large Christmas brunch I had each December, I would display all of my unused gifts in the attic. As people arrived, I would whisper to selected friends and family that they should go up to the attic and pick something.

When I told my siblings of my plan, they immediately and unanimously nixed it.

"Mom already worries about you and your business. If you do this, she'll assume that you're not making enough money to buy Christmas gifts, and she'll worry even more."

They were absolutely right. Even though my business was doing well, that is exactly how my mother would have interpreted the situation. So I re-thought the re-gifting.

Another incident caused her to have to do some re-thinking. For some reason, Mom decided that I liked the Middle-Eastern dish called bazila, a tomato-based stew with meat and whole green peas, often served over rice. Aunt Martha made it almost every Monday night for years. After I moved into my own apartment, she would still call each week to remind me to stop by to have some bazila — and take some home for later.

I hate bazila.

The only way I can stomach green peas is straight from the pod. I'm not sure why Mom thought I liked it; I had never expressed a preference for it, but for years I acted the dutiful son and ate my bazila.

One Monday, after a particularly bad day, I momentarily lost control and blurted out, "I hate bazila." My mother responded in her stern mother persona, "No, you don't. You love bazila!"

At that point, my brother Bob decided to squeeze through the fissure I had created in family solidarity. "And I hate shish barak."

Mom had decided that Bob liked the Lebanese dish composed of meat ravioli cooked in yogurt, and made it for him on his birthday every year.

"No you don't. You love shish barak!"

Luckily, my mother was flexible enough to withstand this attack on her secure world.

But she never asked me to read a contract.

Another birthday with Mike, Mariann and Franny

Chapter Twenty-Nine

A Classic Romance

It was a classic romance. He was the quintessential city boy: grew up on concrete, Catholic, ethnic, handsome despite a hooked nose, swarthy, and no better than he should be. She was a farm girl, literally, with blonde good looks, feet in the soil, Croatian, independent, Presbyterian (sometimes), and all the homey virtues.

It was a match made in heaven.

The real question was, "Could it survive on Earth?" As Tevye maintained, "A fish may love a fowl, but where would they build a home." There were adjustments to be made, so they made them. Luckily, both of them were intelligent, hard working, and gutsy, with a great sense of humor.

My oldest brother Dick met his wife Shirley at a summer course in computers. These were the early, room-filling units that spewed cards and made funny noises. (The computers, that is, not Dick and Shirley.) They were both there to develop an employable skill, which each of them lacked for different reasons. They never really worked very much in the computer industry. In fact, for years, Dick had to rely on his secretary, and later his IT department, to meet his computer needs.

He had grown up in Pittsburgh's Hill District. He was attending Duquesne University during the regular year. Shirley was fresh off the farm. The classic B movie scenario would have had him "take advantage" of her, and then toss her off to some unknown but dire fate. Instead, they fell in love.

In another B movie, this is the point at which the audience would have oohed and aahed and melted. As the closing credits played over romantic music, they would probably argue over which lead was cuter, or likely to be the bigger star.

Dick and Shirl played to tougher audiences. There were my mom and dad, later to become Shirley's biggest boosters, but at this point having real questions about age and compatibility. There were the siblings, bound to be jealous of the attention and her seeming self-assuredness. There was the obstacle of cousins, uncles and aunts, friends old and new, to be overcome.

And there was Grampa.

Grampa Rashid lived with us. When we were younger, he had seemed to recover from a long period of mourning for his wife who had died very young. He talked to us, took us places, and would even play games with us, hiding Life Savers or bags of Planter's Peanuts on his person as he returned home from work each day, and allowing us to climb all over him trying to find them. (Hint: They were usually in his vest pocket.)

As he grew older, he naturally became more and more sedentary. He would take the bus down Fifth Avenue to open the bar each morning, return home about noon, and then sit in his chair in the corner of the living room in front of the TV, immobilized for the rest of the day, except for meals. The younger siblings only knew him as a gruff old man, and typically missed the periodic twinkle in his eyes.

He was a strong man, possessing both great physical strength and great strength of character. His presence was pervasive. He seemed always to know when we had done something stupid. He could convey, with a simple look or a grunt, his approval or disapproval.

It came time to introduce Shirley to our grandfather.

Dick brought her to the house, entered the living room, and stood before my grandfather's chair. Unlike most of our friends, Shirley was able to mask her trepidations well. She might have been scared to death by Rashid, but she didn't show it for a minute. This was obviously one gutsy broad. Dick introduced Shirley.

In Arabic, my grandfather questioned his namesake grandson. "Is she Lebanese?" Dick replied with some of the little Arabic he knew, "La!" (No!)

Grampa's response came in English, "Shit."

I know, I know, neither graceful nor erudite. But with his Arabic accent it sounded less like an expletive than it did like a sigh or groan. And we were so used to hearing it utter forth from his lips that we

157

regarded it as nothing more than a mild statement of disapproval.

Came the next question, in Arabic, "Is she Catholic?"

And Dick's Arabic reply, "La."

Yet again in English, "Shit."

With his rusty Arabic, and his embarrassment over my grandfather's English vocabulary, Dick could barely make out the next question.

"Well then, what is she?"

"Croatian," responsive, but not very informative.

Smiles and a general cheering up.

In English: "I speak dat language!" Actually, my grandfather spoke seven or eight languages that he had picked up in a long and varied career. To my knowledge, they included Arabic, English, French, Yiddish, Polish, Italian, and now, it seemed, Croatian.

He said something to Shirley in Croatian. She replied in English, "I'm sorry, Mr. Kail; I know you're speaking Croatian, but I don't remember any."

In English, "Shit!"

It took Shirley about a year to become my grandfather's favorite. She did it by the simple act of presenting him with his first great-grandchild, a boy-child. From this point until his death several years later, Grampa almost fawned on Shirley, sometimes just holding her hand, other times calling on the phone (I never even knew he knew how to dial a phone) and asking, "How's da boy?"

Despite years of faithful care on the part of my mother and Aunt Martha, as his health began to fail, it was Shirley who my grandfather most frequently requested.

• • •

Dick and Shirley had eloped a few days before his nineteenth birthday. Their marriage was "regularized" by the Church in a graceless ceremony at Epiphany Church.

A few years ago, we celebrated their fiftieth anniversary. By then, their marriage had successfully navigated so many contrasting opinions and preferences, so many compromises and acceptances, we have begun to think it might last.

They had shared so much. Shirley loved to plant green things. Dick loved to walk on green things and hit golf balls. Dick loved to play cards. Shirley loved it that she was carded at bars and clubs into her thirties. A former athlete, Dick loved to watch football. Shirley loved the personal time this provided her.

They decided to build a home, so they entered into negotiations. Shirley, the former farm girl, wanted lots of land, with room to roam and grow things. If permitted, Dick would have preferred to build on a concrete slab in a city neighborhood with easy access to a supermarket, a liquor store, a bookstore, and a cigar store — and maybe some houseplants. The compromise: they built on five acres in a wooded area that had formerly been part of a farm. Dick bought Shirley a small tractor as an anniversary gift.

It is what they hold in common that probably holds them together. They both grew to love music, especially opera and the symphony. They both love theatre. They both love good food and the making of it. They love to read, and travel, and entertain. And they both place a great deal of importance on family.

They also know when it's time to leave each other in peace.

A classic romance? Made in heaven? Who dreams up these things? My personal judgment is that we are not so much dealing with a classic romance here, as we are meeting up with a couple of classy people.

*Dick and Shirley's
Anniversary
"We have begun to think
it might last."*

Chapter Thirty

The House of Mafood

F amily legend has it that, when Grampa Rashid returned to Lebanon to get the rest of the family, his youngest brother remained behind. No explanation was given, and it wasn't a burning question in Pittsburgh.

In fact, it wasn't a question at all in Pittsburgh until many years later, when we found out he existed.

It all started when I returned home from a debate tournament one Saturday night and saw the message light blinking on my telephone answering machine. I hit the "play" button and my Aunt Martha's voice informed me that my mother said I had to be at dinner on Sunday evening.

Now, this did not sound like my mother. She was much more likely to suggest or hint obliquely. I could tell from my aunt's tone, however, that wasn't the case here. This was a full-blown command performance.

I appeared for Sunday dinner at the appropriate time, in appropriate clothes, expecting an explanation. That's when I found out. Not only had my great-uncle remained in Lebanon, his youngest son had later emigrated to Brazil, where he had married well. He was now in Pittsburgh, accompanied by his wife's niece, who wanted to meet "the Kail men."

This sounded serious, even ominous. I felt like hamburger. I half-expected the girl to check my teeth and inspect my hooves. But that only lasted for a moment. Actually, I found it interesting that I had a relative in Brazil (a relation this close was considered immediate family), and looked forward to talking with them and adding to the collection of family stories. This was not as easy as it sounds.

I had noticed the blank look on his face (Let's call him Michael) while Mom explained the circumstances. It turns out he didn't speak English, only Arabic and Portuguese. She (Let's call her Irene.) spoke

Arabic, Portuguese, French and Latin. Notice the word "English" doesn't appear on either of these lists.

I recalled some of my Arabic, some of my scholastic French (reinforced by travel in Europe), and an amazing amount of my high-school Latin, reinforced by my years as an altar boy. Essentially, Irene and I became the interpreters for the group.

She was delightful.

We sat close and attempted to field the questions flowing in either direction. He was married to her aunt, and she was living with them. He and his wife owned a sports clothing factory in Sao Paulo. Yes, she had graduated from college; this trip was part of her graduation gift. No, they would only be staying until the end of the week.

Occasionally, when the questions slowed or there was interaction in the groups, Irene and I would share a moment. She had a wonderful sense of humor.

At one point, the inevitable question arose. Aunt Genevieve, who had just discovered she had another first cousin, asked Irene what "house" she belonged to. Her Uncle Mike was obviously from the House of Zennie, but it turns out that her father was of the "House of Mafood."

From there, it began to break down into a scene from a Marx Brothers movie.

Uncle Joe. understanding very little of the interchange, hears "Mafood" and thinks he hears "Mulfoof," (stuffed cabbage). He asserts proudly, "I love to eat that stuff."

Aunt Gen hearing "Mafood" asks if Irene is related to Cousin Josephine from Pittsburgh. ("I'm pretty sure she's a Mafood.")

Aunt Philomena is just so happy at discovering two new cousins that she sits between Michael and Irene and alternately pets his shoulder and her wrist.

Aunt Martha appears to let us know that dinner is ready.

And Mom is busy giving each one of her sons "The Look," which, in this case, translates into, "One of you has to invite them to dinner at your house. It's expected. What will they think? And I want them to know my children are successful."

Meanwhile Bob and Dick, accurately interpreting Mom's glance, are assiduously avoiding it, in the hope I will be forced to provide the dinner invitation. To Mom's great relief, I did. Michael and Irene stopped by for dinner two or three days later. It was an excellent evening. The smaller group made for clearer communication. Irene and I definitely communicated.

We felt a real connection, I'm sure of it. She was attractive, funny, smart, well traveled, and had rich relatives. She left that Thursday. In the movies, five days and two meetings are enough to fall in love at first sight.

But not in real life.

Who knows what might have happened in a week?

Chapter Thirty-One

The Culinary Arts

The American palate, often shaped by hamburgers and french fries, hot dogs with onions and relish, and bad pasta, underwent a major change in the mid-twentieth century. It might have been caused by greater affluence and the availability of a wider variety of fruits, vegetables, herbs, and spices; or it could be the result of all of the members of the armed services who served abroad and returned home with a taste for "exotic" foods; or it might even have been instigated by the increased migration to America from countries other than Britain, Germany, Ireland, and Italy. Perhaps it was a combination of all of these trends. There is a whole collection of plausible explanations for America's broadening tastes in food.

My personal explanation was my godmother, Mrs. Foutine Samreny. Other ethnic cuisines, especially from central Europe, were celebrated by their native cooks, many of whom worked in the Pittsburgh mills. But they seldom crossed over. Foutine Samreny managed to cross the line into popular consciousness.

The Samrenys and their "restaurant" survived the one-two punch of the Great Depression and the Volstead Act (that almost spelled an end to the American experiment). Immigrants like Mr. and Mrs. Samreny proved how resilient their newly developed American spirit actually was. They combined a sense of adventure with an entrepreneurial spirit, and opened illegal businesses all over the country. Black markets, neighborhood books, speakeasies, any number of these illicit enterprises continued to pump money into a staggering economy, far beyond the WPA or the CCC. Eventually we recovered.

Mrs. Samreny and her husband had children to support. Their contribution to America's economic recovery was a restaurant/speakeasy on Webster Avenue in Pittsburgh's Hill District. I have a sneaking suspicion that it was originally envisioned as a bar, with the primary emphasis on alcohol. In the Lebanese culture, however, one never served alcohol unaccompanied by food, so they had to serve something. Luckily, Mrs. Samreny was a wonderful cook.

Eventually, the restaurant called Samreny's became moderately famous in the local area and beyond, although the emphasis was now on food rather than drink. Joining with similar Middle Eastern establishments throughout the Northeast — there was even a Polish-Lebanese restaurant outside of Philadelphia — it illustrated for Americans that pasta and pizza were not their only choices in ethnic foods.

The Samrenys went on through Prohibition and the Depression, Mrs. Samreny cooking and her children serving wonderful Arabic dishes. Her husband Walter contributed as well. He sat on a stool by the door and collected for the food and drink as the patrons departed.

Among those patrons were David L. Lawrence and his Democratic cronies, triumphant in their win over the Republicans for the office of Mayor of Pittsburgh. His victory allowed the Democrats to displace the Republicans as the primary force in city government, their influence lasting to the very day this story is being written — and probably even as it is read.

When Mrs. Samreny saw the coming of the Pittsburgh Renaissance, with its accompanying deconstruction, she considered closing the speakeasy-turned-restaurant, or so says family legend. Davey Lawrence was among those who dissuaded her. She left the Hill District site, and moved to Baum Boulevard in Shadyside, where she remained until her death in the seventies. Her two sons, my cousins Chuck and Johnny, tried to maintain the business, but could never quite match the consistent quality of their mother. The restaurant closed several years after her death.

Samreny's not only introduced "exotic" dishes to American taste buds, it acted as the wedge that opened the crack through which other ethnic cuisines poured. No longer were Americans limited to diners, steakhouses, and pseudo-French or quasi-Italian restaurants. And, fortuitously, these new exotic cuisines came along at the same time as enrollments in American colleges and universities increased exponentially, providing a ready market with a more adventuresome palate: yogurt, shish kebab, rice with pine nuts, kibbee, tabouleh, baba ganoush, and so on. Eventually, the choice expanded to include kung pao chicken, tapas, pastitsio, sushi, miso, tamales, chile rellenos, curries, plantains, and a whole atlas of dishes from other countries.

And that's how my godmother changed America's tastes — literally.

Of course, at the same time (or even earlier) the West Coast had undergone a similar palate-stretching with the coming of the oriental workforce. There is a story told about the origins of Chinese cuisine in California. It seems that one night a bunch of drunken miners in San Francisco decided to sample this Chinese food they had been smelling in the work camps and Oriental restaurants

Unfortunately for the Chinese restaurateur they chose to bless with their custom, it was about 3 a.m., and he had been closed for hours. Besides, he was almost out of food.

As the miners importuned and threatened him, he recalled his homeland practice of beggars being fed by carrying a bowl from door to door, collecting scraps from multiple houses. Fearful of the drunken crowd, he simply mixed together his leftovers, added a light sauce, heated it, and served the result in bowls. The miners loved the dish. They demanded to know its name, so they could order it again. Thinking quickly, the restaurant owner replied it was "chop suey," not giving them the loose English translation: "beggar's hash."

I'm sure Mrs. Samreny, never even heard of "beggar's hash."

• • •

I have mentioned elsewhere that my maternal grandmother was a famous cook in the Arabic community in Dayton, Ohio. She taught me to cook many Middle-Eastern dishes, and awoke in me a love of cooking — I had already developed a love of eating. She was not the only one, however, other Lebanese parents insisted that their children — male and female — learn at least subsistence-level cooking before leaving home.

In the Lebanese-American culture, there was no stigma attached to a man cooking. In fact, many of the men were better cooks than their wives, and would occasionally illustrate their expertise by preparing dinner. For example, while I consider myself a good cook, I consider my brothers Bob and Dick exceptional cooks (of course, so do they).

In our family, one of the rites of culinary passage involved yogurt. In an Arabic household, a yogurt-maker was simply a large pot — more complicated versions would eventually inspire envy among the effete and elite. You poured in the milk (preferably beginning to "turn"), heated it, and added the "starter," a skim from the last batch that acted as a germ to initiate the yogurt-making process. Each time you made yogurt, you skimmed some of the starter for the next batch.

Everyone I ever met who made yogurt this way — which is to say every Arab-American I knew — stored this "starter" in a clean mustard jar. The practice was puzzling, but nevertheless universal. And, when a child left the family home — to get married, God willing — he or she would be given some "starter" in one of these sacred vessels to take to the new home to initiate his or her own strain of yogurt.

I eventually developed a vision of my great-grandmother, leaving Lebanon to travel to her new country, clutching the primordial mustard jar full of starter between her more-than-ample breasts. Of course, she travelled on a ship full of Arabic immigrants, all of whom probably clutched their own mustard jars.

My mother, being both a good cook, and a good mother, gave each of us a part of our legacy and our heritage as we left home for our first apartments: a mustard jar of yogurt starter with which to start our own line. This was all fine and good, except that I burned one of the early batches of yogurt I attempted, thereby killing off the starter. Before I could surreptitiously replace it somehow, my brother Bob, in an ongoing sycophantic attempt to curry parental favor, squealed to my mother. She waited a long time — for me to prove both my sense of responsibility and my appreciation of my heritage — before replacing it.

As for Bob, I intend to get even some day.

*Dick and I
in the kitchen at
Our Lady of Victory
Maronite Catholic Church*

Chapter Thirty-Two

They Use More Incense

In several chapters of this narrative, I mention the Maronite Church — more accurately, the Maronite Catholic Church. It might be interesting to elaborate. Once again, the analysis provided here is more personal, or perhaps "familial," than historical, the result of more than a half-century of stories and interactions.

First insight: There are actually more than twenty "Catholic" churches, many of them more ancient than the "Roman" Catholic Church (with which Americans are most familiar). In the old days, we often called them "Rites," as if the only differences involved were those of ritual. Even now, you might hear an occasional reference to the "Eastern Rites." But it is more proper to call them "Churches."

Many of them have a cognate Orthodox church, but they are different from the Orthodox churches, basically because the Catholic churches remain loyal to the pope.

If you have heard of any of them, you have probably heard of the Byzantine Rite, or the Byzantine Catholic Church. There are, however, many others, and they are often associated with a national entity. For example, the Byzantines were originally Greek; the Maronites are most often Lebanese; the Ruthenians are primarily Russian; and the Copts tend to be Syrian or Egyptian.

The predominance of the "Roman Catholic Church" — sometimes called the "Latin Rite" or the "Latin Church" — in the Western Hemisphere is due simply to Christopher Columbus and the permanent settlements that eventually grew out of his explorations. Some scholars feel that the much earlier Phoenician explorations included New England and reached as far inland as Michigan and Minnesota. If that is true, and permanent settlements had resulted from them, we'd all be Maronites. It was simply an accident of history that the Roman Catholic European countries created the first permanent settlements.

To American Catholics raised in the Latin Rite, Maronites might seem strange or exotic on several levels, both subtle and obvious. First of all, we are often reminded that the Maronite liturgy, at least the Consecration, is celebrated in Aramaic, "the language that Christ spoke," not the Latin that shaped the Roman Catholic Church. The Maronite Church is named after St. Maron and formed from the Antiochean Christians. Both Maronites and Latins follow roughly the same order of service.

There are differences, but we Maronites tend to look toward those things that unite us rather than divide. For instance, the Maronite Church is proud of the fact that it has never had a schism with Rome, and has always been loyal to the pope, even during the time Lebanon was ruled by the Ottoman Turks.

It is in what can be called the accidental differences that the most interesting contrasts can be seen. The Maronites still have a fascination with liturgy that was lost in the Latin Rite, to a great extent, after Vatican II. My Aunt Martha breaks it down to the basics: "The Maronites use a lot more incense."

There is another "accidental" phenomenon that is more reflective of culture than theology. Much of the Catholic Church in the U.S., especially the Northeast, had its origins in the Irish migrations. Even the later waves of Italian and Middle European immigrants were unable to impact the defensiveness, intellectual bent, and somewhat "austere" spirit that characterized the Irish Catholic Church in New York, New England, and the mid-Atlantic states. Probably because there was such persecution, both here and in the old country, Catholic parishes were often suspicious of, rather than welcoming to, strangers.

Not the Maronites. They warmly welcomed anyone who showed up for liturgy. They would approach them after Mass, show them around the church, and invite them to share a meal. The "corporate culture" was more closely akin to the Hispanic church of the Southwest: warm and welcoming.

I once took a friend, Sister Mary, to a liturgy at my brother/cousin Mike's parish. We had never been there before. After Mass, several people stopped by and began with the question, "Is this your first time in our church." They then invited her to the parish breakfast. She looked at me and said, "The church was full. How did they know?" I just smiled.

Our family has always had an odd relationship with the local Maronite parish. Originally, my Grandfather Rashid was very close to the parish, St. Anne's, and its most famous pastor, Monsignor Basil. Seemingly, Rashid was one of the community patriarchs. I think we began to grow apart after my grandmother died and he became a bit of a recluse for several years.

The "separation" was compounded when my father and his brother married outside the local Maronite community. And it was cast in stone when the kids began attending Epiphany School, with all of its parish responsibilities that took us away from St. Anne. We didn't sever the ties totally, however. The family often supported the Maronite parish as well as the Latin one, and we sometimes served the altar at St. Anne as well.

St. Anne parish was much like the country in which its roots lay. On the surface, everyone supported each other and seemed to get along well. In the face of an outside attack, the membership would show a united front. There was sometimes, however, a layer of "backbiting" and pettiness just below the surface.

My mother and aunt, for example, were never quite part of the "in crowd." There was still some slight stigma attached to their origins in Dayton. The fact that Edith Michaels, a real force in the parish, was one of my mother's best friends helped prevent things from getting too unpleasant.

It was ironic that Mike was the only Maronite vocation the parish ever produced, although there were a couple of priests who had switched to the Latin Rite. As the Kail name became more recognized, and was often associated with the Maronite community, the parish became more accepting. Eventually, Dick and I once again became close to the pastor and the parish.

When Dick formally rejoined the congregation, many of his old friends welcomed him with the invitation to run for parish council. Not ready for the responsibility, Dick declined to run. So they appointed him to council instead.

Originally, North America was a single eparchy (diocese), but, as the number of parishes and members grew, the patriarch, still living in Lebanon, decided to split it into two dioceses. The new border was established partially at the Pennsylvania-Ohio line. Thus, Pittsburgh's Our Lady of Victory is part of The Eparchy of St. Maron of Brooklyn Maronite Catholic Church. My brother-cousin Mike, whose parish is less than a hundred miles away in Youngstown, Ohio, is a member of the Eparchy of Our Lady of Lebanon of Los Angeles Maronite Catholic Church, although the administrative offices are in St. Louis. (Hey, lighten up! I'm just reporting the facts.)

There is an interesting story attached to the translation of St. Anne Parish into Our Lady of Victory Parish.

The horror of World War II arrived in 1941. Like all patriotic Americans, the young people of Pittsburgh's Maronite Catholic community answered the call to serve in the Armed Forces. The family is sacred in Lebanese culture, so we can only imagine the pain involved in the offering of so many children to fight for their adopted homeland.

Seeking some way to instill hope and reinforce the Faith during this dark time, the pastor, Monsignor Basil, made a vow. If all of her children returned safely from the war, he would change the name of the parish to reflect the blessings and protection of Our Lady of Victory.

From this tiny parish of a couple of hundred families, one hundred and fifty-two men and women left to serve. Remarkably, one hundred and fifty-two sons and daughters returned home.

When the parish moved from the Hill District to Brookline during the first Pittsburgh Renaissance, it did so under the name of Our Lady of Victory Maronite Catholic Church.

It's hard to explain our family relationship with the Maronite Catholic Church. As we have grown older, we have "returned" to a closer relationship in many ways. It may simply be a classic case of returning to one's roots. My best attempts at analysis lead me to the conclusion that the church somehow constitutes part of the family identity. It gives us a context, a back story, if you will.

Despite all of the intricacies of the relationship, I have never felt anything but welcome there.

Chapter Thirty-Three

Lebanese-American Culture

For additional insights concerning the material below, please see the chapter called "A Popular History of Lebanon." I will provide the same disclaimer I do there: This is my cultural history, according to my family, gleaned from many years of listening, not necessarily "the" cultural history of the Lebanese-Americans.

By this time, you have probably gained at least a minimal insight into Lebanese culture. This analysis should extend that understanding a bit. Or not.

Lebanon is an Arabic-speaking nation, but not necessarily an Islamic one. The former Maronite Christian plurality has been whittled down through migration and attrition, but it still exerts an influence on the national character.

The "hermit" has a long and storied tradition in Maronite religious history. Many of the early holy men — St. Maron, St. Simon Stylites, and so on — were eremites and spent long stretches alone. Their eremitic tradition differed from the West in that they might very well meet together for prayer and study. They also did not follow the Greek philosophers who split us into mind and heart, intellect and emotions. They saw the human person as more holistic.

On the economic level, the Lebanese are more "Westernized" than their Arab brothers; their land is more fertile and they are more oriented toward trade and finance. This propensity is shared by their American brothers. There is a strong entrepreneurial spirit among first- and second-generation Lebanese-Americans. Many of them developed their own businesses rather than work for others for long periods of time. Even today, they are often characterized as "middlemen" and traders, adding to their somewhat mythic connection with the Phoenicians.

Other characteristic elements are seen frequently in most

Mediterranean cultures. For example, there is a great deal of importance placed on family members and family structure. It is even present in the language, where, for instance, there are four separate words for aunt — one for an aunt who is your mother's sister, another for an aunt who is your father's sister, still another for an aunt who is married to your mother's brother, and yet another for an aunt who is married to your father's brother. The same is true for uncles. The concept of "family" is often broadened to include cousins as immediate family members. Multiple generations, as well as siblings and their spouses and children, often form a single household. Adults who become close to the family are often called "Uncle" or "Aunt."

In my own family, the observation that "they're family" was an explanation in itself. It meant something was owed and expected, and didn't have to be explained.

Another cultural value is hospitality. While I'm not sure that it went so far that you were required to feed your enemy if he showed up at your door — a description often applied to traditional Arabic desert hospitality — it was nevertheless a pervasive influence.

Our house was the gathering place for all of our friends and acquaintances. Ours was the table most frequently expanded to receive guests. We were proud that our friends enjoyed spending time at our home.

Unlike the Islamic Arabic cultures, who eschewed the use of alcohol, Lebanon developed a national drink often rendered in English as araq. It is a very strong, anise-flavored liquor that is distilled several times, so it is extremely pure and causes little hangover. It is clear, looking like water, but adding water causes it to become opaque. My Grandfather Joseph would sometimes entertain us by dipping his forefinger into his glass of araq and lighting it on fire. It took exquisite timing to douse the flame just as the last of the alcohol burned off.

Partially because of its clarity, araq was often called "Tears of the Virgin." The legend maintained that, if she would drink it, she'd cry too.

In my experience, the occurrence of alcoholism in traditional

Lebanese-American culture is very low, especially in the first few generations. For the Lebanese, drinking tends to be a social activity; you seldom see a solitary drinker. And you never have a social gathering without food, so, typically, drinking is accompanied by various sliced breads, vegetables and meats, called a maizeh. Organ meats served raw are a special favorite in a maizeh (although not necessarily my favorite).

Like the Southern Europeans whose migration occurred at roughly the same time, the Lebanese-Americans saw those who preceded them — the Irish, the Germans, the Scots, the English, etc. — as "more American." Unlike the European immigrants, who often formed groups in self-defense, the Lebanese created few formal social or fraternal organizations. Work, church, and family (in the broadest sense) seemed to be enough. Furthermore, as financial "middlemen," who often formed their own businesses, or worked in sales, they didn't provide as much competition for the available manufacturing, construction, and police jobs as did the Southern European immigrants.

While the Lebanese had their share of minor lawbreakers — bookies, speakeasies, and, I suppose, smugglers and fences — they never seemed to create the more formal crime organizations that characterized such groups as the Italians, the Irish, and the Russians — or else they hid it better.

Like the Europeans, the Lebanese gathered in a number of cities and areas, especially in the northeast, and created what were in effect "ghetto" areas that exist even today. They collected in centers such as Brooklyn, Detroit, Massachusetts, Pittsburgh, Youngstown, Cincinnati-Dayton, Los Angeles, St. Louis, the Carolinas, Texas, and so on.

As a group, they were proud of their heritage but not very assertive about their culture. Everyone knew that Danny Thomas was Lebanese, since he was in-your-face about it. But few people realize the Lebanese heritage of stars such as Omar Sharif, Michael Ansara, Tony Shalhoub, and Salma Hayek. And, while there was a short-lived Khalil Gibran craze, there is little equivalent recognition for the literary contributions of Lebanese-American authors such as

Vance Bourjaily and Sam Hazo, or even the late dean of the White House correspondents, Helen Thomas.

But everyone knows their food. From hummus to tabooleh, from kibbee to baba ganoush to baklawa, Lebanese cooking has transformed the American palate.

I have already mentioned the first and most memorable of the Middle Eastern restaurants, Samreny's, run by my godmother. In the Lebanese tradition, my godparents were chosen from among my grandparent's generation. My godfather was John Mowad, who had been one of my grandfather's best friends. My father became the godfather of John's son Tony, who is very active on the international jazz scene.

One final cultural note. The Lebanese, like the Jews, are ethnic Semites, by tradition, sons of Shem, tracing their origins to the Fertile Crescent. Many of the other Arabic speaking countries, especially Egypt, are Hamitic, sons of Ham. I'm not sure if this actually means anything in the real world. Genetic and linguistic analyses yield few scientific certainties.

However, it does seem to have some political relevance. Typically, it was a German journalist, Wilhelm Marr, who began the politicization of what was essentially an anthropological concept. Marr's followers founded the League for Anti-Semitism. While this was by no means the first attack on the Jews, there is a direct line between Marr and the National Socialists — the Nazis of Adolf Hitler.

Chapter Thirty-Four

He Miter Might Not

For many years, I cantored for the baccalaureate Mass each spring during graduation week at Central Catholic High School. That is not as simple as it sounds. What it actually meant was that I had to get 200-300 graduating senior males to sing religious songs, and to do so with volume and fervor.

Why was it so important? I'll never know why, but the parents looked forward to it; and Central was justifiably proud of the dignity and class with which it conducted its ceremonies. Another attribute was brevity. We prided ourselves on keeping them as short as possible. That meant we invited few outside speakers, and those who spoke were reminded to be eloquent and succinct. People actually enjoyed these formal ceremonies.

Baccalaureate, commencement, and honors convocation, all happened within a single week every year. When I became assistant principal, they all fell under my office. For several days in the spring, I became a list-making fury, unable to deal with anything other than these formal ceremonies that would have hundreds of participants and thousands of attendees.

The baccalaureate Mass was particularly special. It filled St. Paul Cathedral with parents, relatives, observers, and beautiful music. The students and faculty, garbed in academic robes, processed into the church from the basement chapel, marching to a full orchestra playing Purcell. The opening hymn would then nearly blow the roof off. Three hundred graduates, accompanied by orchestra and organ, singing at the top of their lungs, had a major impact on the senses.

The problem was to get the students to sing out. As with most male adolescents, when it came to singing religious songs, mumbling was more their métier. Each member of the class seemed to be afraid to sing loudly enough to be heard. I'm not sure whether they were afraid of making mistakes, or whether they just didn't consider it manly; but it was like pulling teeth to get enough volume and accuracy to fill the cathedral with beautiful music.

In order to prepare the graduating seniors, we usually had two one-hour practices in the week between their last day of class and the event itself. Since I was the cantor for the Mass, responsible for leading the singing, it fell to me to teach them the hymns. That meant I had 120 minutes to:

1. Teach them the songs, many of which were unfamiliar;
2. Get them to move beyond the mechanical and discover the beauty of the music;
3. Sing out as loudly as they could without just shouting.

This would usually take approximately 115 minutes. That left us five minutes to polish.

I would wait breathlessly each year for the one moment in the rehearsal when we had repeated a single song so many times that the students would become frustrated. Determined to show me they knew the song, and we could move on to something else, they would practically shout it, enunciating fully, so I couldn't attack that aspect either. When I would finally get them to this point, something almost miraculous would happen. The 300 graduating seniors would like the way they sounded! In full voice, with perfect enunciation and proper religious fervor, they would sail through the remainder of the program.

They became a large male choir, in the tradition of the medieval monks, making beautiful music. And the more they heard how good they sounded, the greater the quality they would require of each other.

Brother James, who was usually the organist for both the rehearsals and the Mass, recognized this moment as well as I did and would throw me a big grin as if to say, "Now we've got 'em!"

There remained only one problem to solve. St. Paul Cathedral was so large that there was more than a second's lag between the organ creating the music in the gallery at the rear of the church, and the students sitting in the front of the church. As the cantor singing in the front of the church, I had to make some reasonable compromise in the timing in order to avoid the dissonance of running ahead or behind the music. And the students had to follow that compromise. The congregation would usually follow the students, although many of them were not singing but listening.

My solution was to take a minute or two to warn the students to "watch my lips. Ignore the organ and watch my lips." It became a bit disconcerting at the podium, where I would sing the verse solo, then wave my arms to lead the congregation in the proper response, while watching all of the students staring at my mouth. I was hard put not to lead them astray by contorting my lips at odd times.

All of this became simply background material one year when Bishop Leonard was the primary celebrant at baccalaureate. We were to create a procession into the church from the basement Lady Chapel, up the steps to the sidewalk, down the side of the church, up the front steps, and in the front door, in the following order: the six altar boys, the bishop with two masters of ceremonies, myself as cantor along with the lector, a large group of priest graduates and pastors who were invited to concelebrate each year, and the faculty, followed by the students. Except for the bishop, all of us marched two-by-two.

This was the same Bishop Leonard who, as chancellor of the diocese, had to try a famous property case all the way to the Supreme Court a quarter of a century before.

When Pittsburgh began its famous Renaissance in the early fifties, there were two churches one block apart. The Church of the Epiphany was solid red brick and marble. The physical facilities comprised the church, the rectory, the school, a large building called the Pittsburgh Lyceum (containing a full gym and library), and a YWCA-like home for professional women (called the St. Regis Home). It was a heavily Irish parish.

St. Peter, the Italian parish, was primarily wood and plaster within. It contained a church, a rectory, a school, and a large outdoor shrine to the Blessed Virgin. There was no room in the master plan of the city for two churches.

We were told that it would cost significantly more to buy the Epiphany than it would to buy St. Peter. Furthermore, it was larger and could accommodate a combined parish. Finally, it was the parish of then Mayor David L. Lawrence.

The parishioners at St. Peter heard only that the Irish parish would survive and theirs would be destroyed. That's all they needed to take it to law, a case that lasted several years and was finally decided by the Supreme Court of the United States, so the tale went.

At every event held by the diocese over this multiyear period, a disgruntled parishioner would picket with a sign reading "Save St. Peter's Church." Pictures of the sign were all over the news when the final decision came in: The bishop is a corporation sole that owned all of the property in the diocese. And down went St. Peter Church.

I guess the picketer was used to showing up at diocesan events, because he continued for several years, eventually changing the sign to read, "Bring back the Tridentine Mass" (i.e., the Latin Mass replaced by the vernacular after Vatican II) and, eventually, "Congressman Coyne is reading your mail."

Thus, on this baccalaureate evening twenty-five years later, when the picket showed up, Bishop Leonard was curious. He squinted and then turned to me to ask, "Hey, Kail, What's that sign say?"

You don't often get a chance to tease a Bishop.

To this day, I feel a bit embarrassed about what I glibly answered, "It says, 'Save St. Peter's Church'!"

Bishop Leonard, always a "regular guy," responded with a guffaw so large that his miter — the pointed hat worn by a Catholic bishop for formal ceremonies — fell off his head and went rolling down the street. Caught by the wind, it rolled over and over, rather than in a straight line. Most members of the procession weren't aware of the problem. Perhaps caught up in their own self-importance and robes of various types, they seemed oblivious.

But we had taught the students well. A bishop in need overruled almost everything else. The procession halted for approximately ten minutes, while almost half of the processing students in their caps and gowns, broke ranks and chased the bishop's miter down the street. Three boys proudly returned it to a smiling bishop shortly thereafter. The smile on the face of the bishop required a corresponding smile on the face of the principal, who might otherwise have meted out discipline for causing chaos.

The adventure ended when someone finally thought to head up to the organ loft to let the orchestra know of the delay. They had played every piece in their repertoire during the hiatus. They started over again.

As soon as they read out my name at Duquesne's commencement, dad got up and left.

Chapter Thirty-Five

Dialectical Me

I 've always been fascinated by dialects: foreign dialects, American regional dialects, BBC English, General American Dialect, they all challenge the mind, the ear, and the tongue. I think it began on the Hill where, on any given day, you could easily hear dialects as diverse as Yiddish, American Black, Italian, Greek, and Arabic within the same conversation.

I have also found that the ability to mimic dialects — which I developed almost unconsciously — is a valuable skill set. Over the years, I have done stage shows in dialect, entertained friends, and shot commercials.

One of the things I've discovered is that, to create what sounds like an "accurate" dialect, your mimicry needn't be totally spot on. You simply need to identify a few key sounds and imitate them accurately. The listener's ear will fill in the rest. Of course, this doesn't fool the linguist, but a linguist is seldom involved in the process anyway.

Another thing I have discovered about dialects is that, no matter how much we protest to the contrary, most of us equate certain dialects with inferiority in intelligence, or social status or cultural development, etc. Whether the accent is ethnic, regional, socio-economic, or class-related, the listener makes a judgment. And it's usually negative, and it's usually out of fear — fear that they will not understand and be made to feel stupid, fear of the "other," fear of mingling with a different class. Sometimes they simply regarded it as quaint. Residents of the Hill District, and other centers of immigration, were sometimes patronized on this basis.

Let's face it. People sometimes use speech patterns as an equivalent for education, (and, therefore, class), and just like color, race, ethnicity, or sexual orientation, it is sometimes a source of scapegoating and discrimination. When a kid from Brooklyn gets an education, one of our expectations is that he will no longer sound as if he's from Brooklyn. But, unlike those other causes of discrimination, we can do something about our speech, not as a mask to hide behind, but as a mark of learning.

I'm perfectly willing to admit that not everyone makes these types of judgments, but it is prevalent enough that, when I was teaching, and also coaching speech and debate, I spent time working on my students' dialects. I would tell them that, right or wrong, they would be judged by their speech. They should learn the difference between formal and informal speech, just as they'd study the difference between formal and informal writing or fashion.

For instance, if you were out with your friends playing football, you wouldn't call out, "Cast the ovoid in my direction." (At least, not if you grew up in my neighborhood, and not more than once.) It would simply be something like, "Throw me the ball!" Or simply "Here!"

And if you were at tea with the bishop (although I never met anyone who had tea with the bishop), it would be inappropriate to request, "Hey, Bish, lay one a them crumpets on me, will ya?" (Now that I think about it, I could probably name several friends and family members who might do exactly that — just for fun.)

Occasionally a student would protest that he wasn't going to be "fake." I would try to explain that, if he learned the skill, it wasn't fake, any more than it was fake for him to learn to hit a fastball or drive a car. It was simply a skill to be learned. Most of them understood, and a surprising number later thanked me.

I was rehearsing the role of Emil in the Rodgers and Hammerstein classic *South Pacific.* We were intensely rehearsing one of the scenes where Nellie visits Emil and they talk about his background and the necessity to leave France after killing a villain in a fight. This obviously suggested a French accent, and for the first few weeks of rehearsal, we had concentrated on developing a realistic one, and one that was not Parisian at that.

But something was wrong. All of us realized it, although none of us had broached the subject. We were singing the thoughtful "Twin Soliloquies" when it dawned on me. I looked at Nellie and she seemed to have the same realization at the same time. It was probably a single word that tripped the trigger in both of us.

The trouble with doing an old "war horse" like *South Pacific* or *Oklahoma* is that most of your audiences have probably already seen at least a movie or a TV production, or even a live performance, and have certain expectations. When you think of The King and I, for example, it's almost impossible not to hear Yul Brynner in the title role. And the first few bars of *Oklahoma* — "There's a bright golden haze on the meadow" — inevitably ring out in Gordon MacRae's rich baritone, at least in my mind.

South Pacific had opened on Broadway starring the operatic icon Ezio Pinza in the male lead. It was a groundbreaking experiment and it worked wonderfully. When the time came to shoot the movie, another Italian icon starred as Emil, Rossano Brazzi. To compound the illusion, his voice was dubbed by a third Italian, singer Georgio Tozzi. (As I write this, Tozzi's female counterpart, Marni Nixon — the voice of Peggy Wood in *The Sound of Music*, Natalie Wood in *West Side Story*, Audrey Hepburn in *My Fair Lady*, and so many others — has died, silencing one of the most supple and beautiful voices of the screen.)

The problem with my interpretation was that I was singing the role in a relatively accurate French dialect, yet the "world" was trained to expect an Italian dialect; more than that, a northern Italian dialect. So that's what we decided to give them, and they seemed to accept it without a problem.

I later discovered the source for my northern Italian dialect. I was running in a summer stock comedy called Avanti! I played an Italian guide of questionable sexual orientation. One night, I received a note in my dressing room that the family of one of my former students was in attendance that night. He had been a favorite student, and I had been invited to one or two social functions at his home. His father was a doctor of some fame in research circles, who had emigrated from Italy several years before.

All of a sudden, I began to blush. It continued until it developed into an actual flush. (Given my normal complexion, this was extreme.) I was realizing that the northern Italian voice I was hearing

185

in my head when I developed the dialect was that of the doctor who was waiting to watch me on stage tonight as I played him.

Of course he didn't realize it then, but I was convinced that he would immediately hear his own "voice," and be offended that I was making fun of him. I was mortified. I'm sure I stumbled through most of my lines that night, not really on top of my game.

The note indicated that the family planned on stopping back after the performance to say hello, and even invited me to join them for a late supper or a drink. I told one of the other actors about my dilemma, and, instead of sympathy, I got laughter.

"He will never in a million years make the leap you're so worried about," she said, and rushed off to tell the other actors. So they could watch my discomfiture as the family approached.

As they entered the dressing room, I was standing there, prepared to offer an abject apology. The first thing out of the doctor's mouth was, "What a wonderful Italian accent you do, I felt like I was at home." Talk about anticlimactic.

From the fact that I could perform dialects, people often extrapolated to the conclusion that I could understand them more easily as well. I guess it's possible, but I think it was sometimes a ploy not to have to deal with the issue. Wherever I worked, if someone answered the phone and heard broken English on the other end, the call would be forwarded to me to deal with, no matter who or what the person was requesting.

I began this essay talking about the involvement of the mind, the ear, and the tongue in the process of creating dialects. There is some evidence that it involves more of the body as well.

Some years ago, I received a call from a producer who was shooting a commercial and wanted me to do the voiceover the next day. I told him to fax me a script and I would learn it overnight. He replied that I wouldn't be on camera, so I could just pick it up the next morning when I went to the studio.

As I entered the studio, the receptionist handed me the script and directed me to the suite where they were shooting. When I got there, I saw the producer, (with whom I had worked several times), the tech person (who had just finished recording a radio program I occasionally did), and the director. I had never met him. We talked a bit about what he wanted and he pointed me toward the recording booth.

I entered the booth, donned the headset; we set the levels, and began. The ad was for late-night TV, a commercial for a set of tapes on how to dance the Lambada. I cracked up the first time through. I thought the Lambada craze had gone the way of disco. Evidently not in the Miami market.

When we finished the first few takes, I noticed the three of them deep in discussion, and soon the director called me over.

"These guys say you do dialects. I didn't look at your resume. Do you do Hispanic."

I hesitated, "Well, yes, but do you really want to fake a dialect?

And so, he stated the obvious, "It won't sound fake if you're any good."

I headed back to the booth and got ready to try it in a Hispanic dialect I had "perfected" at City Theatre a few years before. I lowered my pitch, and deepened my voice. I rolled my "R's," and changed my cadence, all the little secrets I had learned when I envisioned myself playing Ricardo Montalban. So I began again.

"Dare to dance the forbidden dance ... Dare to dance ..." And I ended with a breathy intonation that I dragged out for effect — "the Lambadaaa!"

When I looked at the guys in the studio, the director gave me a thumbs-up sign; he obviously liked it. By the time I gathered my things and walked over to the console, they were in the middle of a laughing fit. I felt sort of vulnerable, so I challenged, "What's so funny?"

They pointed to the large video monitor and said "Watch!"

I'm not sure whose idea it was, but they had obviously recorded the session on video as well as audio. As they played back the first part, I watched myself reading the script. I sat there with the headset on and calmly laid down the track. When we got to the recording in dialect, it was a bit of a different story.

I had stood to read the Hispanic voiceover. As I talked, my hips swiveled, my shoulders rotated, I gesticulated wildly — all of the physicality that we stereotypically associate with the Anglo playing a Latino. I looked as if I were doing a second-rate Steve Martin.

I guess there is obviously more involved in creating a dialect than the mind, the ears, and the tongue.

I never asked which version they used for the commercial. I didn't want to know.

Chapter Thirty-Six

What the Students Taught Me

I became assistant principal of Central Catholic High School in February, replacing a good friend who had left to become a principal at a different school during the previous December. I continued to teach my classes. Consequently, time was precious.

I had always been one of those teachers who loudly, and with a bit of self-righteousness, bemoaned the fact that schools were structured for the convenience of teachers and administrators, not students. I soon became less adamant about the convenience of administrators. It was one of the busiest times of my life. I had three hundred students graduating in three months. I had to plan commencement, baccalaureate Mass, and the honors convocation in that time, while performing all of my standard administrative and teaching tasks.

I was sitting in my office one day, shuffling graduation lists, grade lists, and so on, when a young student appeared at my door. My secretary stopped him for a moment and then sent him in. He asked some stupid question; I can't remember what it was. But I remember my reaction. I blew him off. Luckily I did it with good humor, but nevertheless effectively. I needed to check those names.

I found myself blushing almost immediately. One month as an administrator, and I had already become a list maker. I was sincerely embarrassed. I called the student back into my office and apologized. I felt noble, he felt confused. He had no idea what I was talking about.

That taught me several things. First, students expected to be treated somewhat shabbily; they were used to it. What did that say about us? Second, you could get away with a great deal in your interaction with students if you did it with good humor. And finally, if I wanted to maintain contact with the students, I was going to have to tell the well-meaning secretary that any time my door was open, allow any student to enter.

I have always thought of myself as a teacher. Even years after leaving the classroom, "teacher" is still the first response that comes to my mind should someone ask me what I do.

But I didn't become a good teacher until I realized that I had a great deal to learn from my students.

It took only a year or so to learn a lot about honesty and respect. At one point, I was performing in a show. It was tech week and we were putting in a lot of late nights. One morning in class, I realized that my late hours the night before had left me with a throbbing headache and an energy level that had bottomed out. I figured, "What do I have to lose." I looked at my class and said, "Look guys, I had a really bad night last night, and I'm not doing very well. So, I don't need any hassles today. OK? Cut me some slack."

They responded by becoming, at least for that day, a model class.

A few days later, I was collecting homework papers from the class when one of the students admitted that he didn't have his. When I asked why, he said he had a major argument with his parents the night before and couldn't concentrate. By this time, the others were listening. He asked me to cut him some slack. He would turn it in tomorrow.

Now I was in a bind.

I had asked a similar favor of them a few weeks ago, and they responded well. Furthermore, he had never been late with homework before, so I trusted he was telling the truth. But, if I granted his extension on this basis, how was I to control the rest of the class? Wouldn't I be inundated with late assignments because they had a "bad night?"

Finally, I decided to talk to the class. I explained my dilemma and asked for suggestions. They looked at each other for a while, somewhat puzzled, since they had seldom been approached on this level. One student finally blurted out, "Why don't you just trust us until we do something wrong."

He was asking for respect, the benefit of the doubt, something we would give a peer or parent as a matter of course. Why not trust the students as well, until they did "something wrong?" So I did. I got burned occasionally, but not as often as you might think.

The students kept underlining this simple lesson year after year. After I became an administrator, I pretty much had the ultimate responsibility for discipline. One morning, "Bill" came huffing into my office, obviously angry and distressed. He told me that "Mr. Smith" had thrown him out of class. This was unorthodox at best; there was a procedure for dealing with a disruptive student, although we seldom needed to use it.

I asked Bill what he had done; he, of course, said, "Nuthin'."

I asked again.

"You're just gonna take his side, anyway."

We talked for a moment, and he ended up admitting that he had been disrespectful to the teacher. He hadn't completed a major assignment and the teacher kept picking at him throughout the class, using him as an example for the other students. By the middle of class, he was standing over Bill making fun of his excuse to the other guys. Bill, feeling cornered, lost control and shouted some things at the teacher. Mr. Smith threw him out of class.

I sat Bill down and worked out a discipline contract with him. It included, among other things, several detentions, a discussion with his parents, and some hours of service. Then Bill left for his next class.

By the way, in more than eight years of developing "disciplinary contracts," only two students ever failed to fulfill their agreement with me.

At the bell, Mr. Smith came stomping into my office, stepping in front of several students as he approached my desk. "Did Bill report to you? What did you do to him?"

I became upset with his arrogance and insensitivity — never, of course, having a problem with these issues myself. I apologized to the waiting students and asked them to stop by later. I turned to confront Mr. Smith. I told him what I had done to Bill, and didn't even try to bring up at that time the procedure he should have followed. He practically shouted at me, "That's not enough. I want him suspended."

And I lost it, although you might not have been able to tell from the level of my voice, as I said, "He's sixteen, he's supposed to be stupid. What's your excuse?"

I was trying to explain, admittedly somewhat arrogantly and insensitively, that it was seldom appropriate or advisable to corner a kid in front of his peers. They don't have the skills to handle it. If the situation wasn't threatening, the teacher should have dropped it until after class. He was the adult.

And ridiculing the kid was never the answer.

Needless to say, it took some discussion to smooth over the face-off. But a little bit of respect in the beginning would have defused the situation, so that it could be dealt with properly.

One other example provides a final insight. For several days, we had been having trouble with fire alarms going off. Since it was a large campus with several buildings, it was impossible to guard every alarm box. In a four-day period, we had to empty the building five times, with all the disruption that entailed.

Everyone had a solution. They ranged from "Ignore them" to "Disconnect the alarms;" from "keep everyone in detention until they identify the perpetrator" to "Call off school for a few days until things cool down."

It seemed to me that stopping the action was more important than identifying which student was setting off the alarms. I suggested to the principal that we hold an assembly and talk to the students. He said, "Fine, you talk to them."

At the assembly, I simply admitted we were stumped. We had almost no way to stop the alarms short of bringing in the police and allowing them to investigate. One boy suggested that we ignore the alarms. I explained that we couldn't do that for reasons of safety. There were a few other suggestions, each more impractical than the last.

I finally said, "Look. I'm simply telling you that we have no solutions, no options, but to continue emptying the building at each alarm. But let me ask this: Is this really funny? Who are the losers here?"

I never asked who did it.

The students quietly filtered out of the auditorium. We never had another false alarm while I was there.

Given my ego, it took me longer than it should have to realize that, because a student knew less than I did, that didn't mean he was less than I was. Yet much of our primary and secondary educational system is built on that presumption. We automatically distrust students. We "discipline" them for not having the skills that we, or their families, or simply time and maturity should teach them.

Don't get me wrong. I think there are bad students just as there are bad teachers, perhaps even because there are bad teachers. And we have to be prepared to deal with them. But to treat all students as if they were untrustworthy and out to put something over on us makes no sense,

Final case in point: At one of our infrequent assemblies, a student made a sarcastic remark loud enough that he was heard several rows away. At most schools, they would have been happy that was the only "disruption." Our students were usually so well behaved that the teachers considered this almost heinous conduct. Several teachers called for major punishment for the student. Others demanded that we cancel the remainder of our assembly program.

What he had done was no worse than you might hear at any movie theater, and that was the problem. The movies had established his standard of behavior in an auditorium setting, not us. So I simply expanded the assembly program, and, at each one, took a minute to explain what type of behavior and response was considered appropriate. We never had another assembly problem.

I know that teaching at Central Catholic exposed me to some pretty select students, at least as regards intellect. Thus, I must acknowledge the fact that I was teaching the "elite," but we had helped make them the elite. I grew up in the Hill District; not all of its denizens were quite so select. Yet, I never met a kid who didn't prize being treated with respect and honesty.

This wasn't some brilliant insight that I alone discovered. The more schools, teachers, and students with whom I interacted, the more I realized that, whatever name they gave it, this concept of respect and trust was at the root of all good teaching.

And that's what the students taught me.

I visit Canevin Catholic High School

Chapter Thirty-Seven

Vietnam

I have never been able to resolve my feelings about the war in Vietnam. In the sixties and seventies I strongly opposed it and participated in several demonstrations. I spoke out against it frequently, alienating some friends and family. As I look back, I'm sure some of the opportunities I exploited were inappropriate, but how do you have an "appropriate" protest?

On the other hand, I have always had guilt feelings about the war. Many of my friends were drafted, and several of them were killed. And how was I to know that I wasn't merely acting out of fear? Would I have been able to go to fight? I would have hoped I had the courage to refuse — and accept the consequences.

As it turned out, I not only had a college deferment, but I also was 4F; and when my draft number was drawn I was in the high 200s.

Years later, I was just as certain of the idiocy of our involvement in the second Gulf War. I am still conflicted about Pakistan and Afghanistan, but how we justified invading Iraq — again — makes me question the conduct of my own government and ask what I could/should have done to oppose it.

Since I had never resolved my feelings about Vietnam, this new round of warfare simply exacerbated my confusion.

I understand that blood is occasionally the cost of protecting our freedoms, but with many of our military expeditions, I could not be sure it was freedom we were protecting and not just oil or image or prestige. What do you do, then, about the people who feel very strongly that they are protecting our basic freedoms?

One thing I resolved to do, as a sort of symbolic gesture, was to try to get some closure, to have the guts to speak to someone who was there. I wanted to try to explain my dilemma, and, in a kind of convoluted act of contrition, ask for some type of informal forgiveness.

I wanted to be sure that someone understood that what I opposed was the war. What I protested was the shortsighted and self-serving conduct of our politicians. What I was demonstrating against was the lies and the deception and the deaths.

Or was that merely camouflage for cowardice?

I know it seems contradictory, but I had great respect and concern for our soldiers.

What I really needed was absolution.

The Vietnam veteran I was closest to was Art. Art was married to my sister/cousin Franny, and we saw each other fairly frequently, even getting together to play poker every few months.

Art is straightforward and no nonsense. An ex-Marine (is any Marine really "ex"?), he tends to see the world in black and white. I figured that, if I could talk to him, and he accepted my explanation, I would rest a bit easier.

I waited for Veteran's Day, struck by its appropriateness. I called Art, hoping he had a few minutes to talk. Unfortunately, I got an answering machine with a mechanical voice saying the typical, "Start recording after the beep."

I wasn't prepared for this; I had steeled myself for an emotional interaction, and this seemed almost anticlimactic. But I was on the phone and the beep had sounded and I either had to speak or hang up. I decided to speak.

I don't really remember what I said, but it began with, "I just wanted you to know ..." I know the message contained words like "respect" and "guts" and "memories."

I don't know what I expected next. I'm not sure if I anticipated that Art would call back, or make reference to the call the next time we were together, or simply ignore it.

Several weeks passed without a response. One Sunday morning we gathered at the house as we did nearly every week. The conversation was about something completely different. Suddenly Mariann's husband Andy looked at me and said, "Oh, I meant to tell you that I got a telephone message from you that was probably intended for Art. I erased it by mistake."

So, I'm still conflicted about Vietnam, but at least I tried.

Chapter Thirty-Eight

Joy and Harry and Bob and Me

These stories are about family, but I must admit I'm sometimes not sure what that means. Rather, I realize that what it means to me is different from the standard definition. It is my experience that, the stronger a family is, the more clear its values and traditions, the more attractive it is. People want to spend time in it, to share in its activities, to become part of it. In the strongest and most generous families, this happens automatically. They incorporate new members into family life.

In my family, this happens on two levels. There are the family members that are "adopted" for a period of need or a period of time. The family offers a support structure based on circumstance and coincidence; and, when the support is no longer needed or circumstances change, the person moves on. Our family had many of this type of family member.

On the other hand, there were adopted family members who, pretty much literally, joined the family. They were loved and treated as family. They were expected at family activities and didn't need an invitation. Their nuclear family was in touch with our family. Perhaps the most telling sign of "adoption" was the treatment by the rest of the family. Essentially, once a "new" member had been fully integrated, he or she would be expected at activities that had no relation to the figure who had introduced them into the family in the first place.

We had several of these members. Thus Uncle Joe's friend, Bill Kulak, became family. As did Bob's friend Arlene, and his housemate of many years, Gerry Dalton.

I don't know if I was in love with Joy Coccodrilli, but I certainly loved her. And for many years I considered her my best friend. Moreover, the family loved her as well, so much so that people sometimes bitched at her, just as they did with the rest of us. Joy became family, so it's important to me that you meet her.

Joy grew up on a small dairy farm in the Pocono Mountains near Scranton, Pennsylvania. While she cherished her roots and her family, in some ways, she quickly grew beyond them. She was extremely intelligent, sensitive, pretty, sexy, competent, and a good listener. She was also short, and, during the time I knew her, kept her dark hair in a pixieish bob that matched the persona she sometimes adopted.

She had gone to a convent school in Scranton. She later said she put up with "some nonsense," but she seemed to get a good education, profit from her experiences, and retain some happy memories. When it came time for college, she decided to major in pharmacy at Duquesne University in Pittsburgh. She later switched her major to English. My brother Bob was also in English at Duquesne, having previously left the seminary.

I'm not exactly sure where, when, or even how Bob and Joy met, but they did meet and began spending a lot of time together. This was a time when college dorms still observed curfews (usually around midnight), so, when Joy and Bob went out, she would often "sign out" for the night, and end up on the couch in our living room. I was seldom home before midnight or 1 a.m. Since she was frequently awake when I came home, and Bob invariably was not, I began looking forward to spending time with Joy.

We talked for hours, which probably means that I talked for hours. Joy would listen empathetically to the outpourings of a self-centered adolescent who was sure of everything. She never seemed impatient; she never cut me off. She listened to all of my jokes and laughed in all the right places. She was only a few years older than I, but seemed immensely more mature, and I'm sure I placed her on a pedestal from which she never fell, even in later years when my evaluations became a tad more objective.

Meanwhile, our two families — the Kails and the Coccodrillis — met each other and found we were cut from the same cloth (i.e., ethnic, conventional, hospitable, religious, family-oriented, etc.). Her mother and my mother hit it off and from then on frequently inquired about each other. This cemented Joy's place in our family.

Even my dad, who seldom recalled even the name of any of my friends, would greet her affectionately, and inquire after her welfare. And Bertha and Dante, Joy's parents, personified unqualified love. Dante and my father even looked alike.

Now come the complications. Joy and Bob seemed to get closer for a while — he even gave her a "pre-engagement" ring, as someone called it, hoping to provide a not-so-subtle push. And then they seemed to drift apart. Poor Bob, it was no longer his relationship; we all had a stake in Joy. I never asked him about their status, I simply maintained my own relationship, as did the family, when they had the chance.

Shortly after graduation, Bob and Harry, another friend from Duquesne, began to share an apartment. Bob and Joy were still in touch; and, like my family and me, Harry also fell in love with Joy. Later, Harry moved into his own apartment, and Bob moved in with Gerry Dalton, another friend. All of us still maintained a relationship of varying degrees of closeness.

After graduation, Bob and Harry began teaching at the same high school in Pittsburgh. Joy also remained in Pittsburgh and began working at one of the local department stores, where she rose quickly through the management ranks. In addition, her brother Don and his wife also moved into the area. (Don and his wife, along with assorted uncles and cousins, just seemed automatically to be part of my family; of course, I never asked them if they wanted to be.)

Harry and Joy began dating.

We were all becoming more and more entwined. Meanwhile, at some point, Harry added the Gallagher family to this agglomeration of friends and acquaintances — Joanne, Arlene, and Bud — friends of his from McKeesport. They were all active in theatre — Harry was a superb pianist – and the circle was completed when Bob and I began to work with all of them at McKeesport Little Theatre.

It's amazing how complex these relationships became, although I'm not sure we ever really thought of them that way. Essentially, we had all become a sort of surrogate family for each other to varying degrees. (Are you beginning to see a pattern?)

Then everything changed, sort of.

Joanne Gallagher became a teacher for the Department of Defense and left to take up her post overseas. Harry, who was still dating Joy, eventually decided to join the DOD as well, and was sent to Okinawa. I took over the lease to his apartment in Shadyside.

Late one night, there was a knock at the door. When I opened it, Joy breezed in carrying a housewarming gift of some wonderful coffee mugs and a sinful strawberry cheesecake. She informed me that, since I had inherited Harry's apartment, I had also inherited her. This was fine with me. We grew a lot closer and this was one of the happiest periods of my life.

The connections continued. Joy became even more a part of the family when she accepted a job at a department store in Dayton, Ohio, and I had the joy of introducing Joy to my mother's family.

A few years later, Harry and Joy decided they wanted to be together, so they married. They lived in New York for a while, and eventually moved to Puerto Rico, and then St. Croix, ultimately adopting a child, Loren.

We all kept in touch through the years; and, for a brief period, Joy's brother Don and I shared a house.

This is an awfully long way to go to get to the heart of this story, which is Joy, but I wanted to show her in context. She was a remarkable, even a unique, person, and her influence is so pervasive that I see it at all stages of my life and in many of my friends. All through this collection of stories she has been on my mind, and I somehow feel compelled to talk about her.

You have probably noticed that I have been using the past tense when speaking of Joy. She was killed in a car accident in 1985. This is not meant to be a sad story, so I wanted to explain that, rather than try to create some type of dramatic climax. I simply want to share Joy with you.

She was remarkable in many ways, and yet, at the same time, was very human. First of all, she brought out the best in people. She didn't demand the best; you simply wanted to be your best when you were with her. I never knew how she did that.

She made connections; she loved to share the people she loved. She was very much a family person, with strong loyalties and a willingness to forgive. But family was a flexible concept; she and I considered each other as family, with all that implied.

She didn't let you fool yourself; she would never expose or embarrass you, but she disliked pretense and would subtly insist that you be yourself. You can imagine what effect this might have on me. I was never as genuine with anyone as I was with her. I grew to very much like the person I was when I was with Joy.

Joy was able to be loving and caring and accepting without giving up a critical sense. She never approved your acts that were hurtful or petty or wrong, but she never withheld her love. Nor did her family, who seemed to accept me with all my flaws, and never seemed to judge. The roots of Joy's personality were obvious.

I gave one of the eulogies at her funeral, and it's almost as if I were anticipating this book.

"She made each of us feel important and central to her life. That was Joy's gift: to make all of us, each of us, feel at home; to feel, in a very literal sense, 'part of the family.'"

Joy and I

Chapter Thirty-Nine

In Conclusion

I have learned several things by writing this book. For example, actions and events that I felt were obvious and straightforward often seemed obscure to other people. As a sort of reality check, I sent several of these stories to various people for comment, and comment they did. Memories differ. Conclusions vary.

It also became clear that, while I often considered myself as a/ the central figure in many of these stories, in actuality I was often peripheral to what occurred. I have amazing guilt feelings about how many of the chapters in this book begin with "I" or "My." I simply have a healthy ego — as if that hasn't become obvious.

I was a bit surprised to find out that many of my siblings and relatives had come to the exact same conclusions about certain issues as I had, even though I had been sure they thought differently. We had just never discussed them. And it amazed me how closely our analyses had followed the same lines of reasoning and reached the same conclusions. Boy, are they smart!

If you have read these lines — and between them — you probably know a lot about me. Don't let it go to your head. And in a completely unjustifiable, and perhaps even reprehensible way, I have also told you a lot about my family. I'm not sure I have a right to do that, although this book is the result of a desire to celebrate the richness of the family history, not to expose its idiosyncrasies and hold it up to ridicule.

In those chapters less directly concerned with the family, I hope you will forgive my presumption. They are there not so much because you have a need to read them. They are there because I have a need to write them, perhaps to own them, to say them, to share them.

It dawns on me that you might like to know what happened to the members of the family, at least the ten siblings in my generation.

I'm proud of all of them; and, try to hide it as I might, I think they are exceptional. Thank you, Dave and Helen and Joe and Martha. So, the ten children in the family have reached the following "milestones:"

- Richard married Shirley, and they had David. Dick became a Divisional Superintendent of Claims for State Farm. Retired.

- Robert became associate dean of engineering at Carnegie-Mellon University. Retired.

- Eugene became handsome, and then the assistant principal at Central Catholic High School and eventually ran his own communications and marketing group for twenty-plus years.

- Michael was ordained and is now a Maronite chorbishop with a parish in Ohio.

- Mariann married Andy and they had Casondra and Heather. Mariann is a psychologist and an adjunct teaching at a local college.

- Frances married Art, and they had Suzanne and Michelle. Frances is a senior unit manager at Federated Investors.

- Judith has a position of major responsibility with the Allegheny County Health Department.

- Theresa married Tom. They are the parents of Steve, Nicole, and T.J. Theresa serves on Pittsburgh's City Council.

- Rosanne married Ted, and they had Zack. Rosanne is the assistant executive director of Intermediate Unit 3, an educational unit of the State of Pennsylvania Department of Education.

- Patricia recently accepted a position as senior consultant for a national resource company.

In many ways, this is the story — these are the stories — of any second- or third-generation immigrant family, although I/we have been luckier than many. While there are tensions and disagreements among the family members, most of us are willing to get over it for the sake of the family. There is a caring among the family members. That is not necessarily unique. What is almost unique is the fact that we are still together. We gather regularly; we call to check on each other; we support each other. To say that I am profoundly grateful seems so little.

One of the things I love best about the family is simply that we know each other — four generations of us. If God and Aunt Mart cooperate, it may eventually be five.

One final observation: Before writing this book, I would have maintained, quite sincerely, that I was not worried about what happened to my name after I was gone. I wasn't hung up on being remembered, and was actually pretty much resigned to being forgotten, even by my family.

I have come to realize that, if the truth were known, I desperately want to leave some type of legacy. I want people to laugh at something I said; I want my family to miss my contributions, to think about me, no matter the context. I want my former students to recall what a wonderful teacher I was, and members of the audience to recall their favorite performance of mine. True or not.

I surprise myself. Yet I want the record to show I was here, that I made a difference, that there was a significance to my life.

Oh, well, I guess you can't have everything.

Top: Bob, David, Dick and I on Wedding Day

Bottom: Bob, Dick and I surround mom (waiting for assignments)

Afterword

Once there was a fourth-grader who received a book from his teacher on which he was to write a book report. It was a book about penguins. His book report consisted of a single sentence. He wrote, "This book told me more about penguins than I wanted to know."

I hope I'm not guilty of the same offense as the author of that book.

Pittsburgh
October 24, 2015
On my Birthday

Made in the USA
Middletown, DE
25 May 2022

66250331R00116